CONTENTS

Helion & Company Limited
Unit 8 Amherst Business Centre, Budbrooke Road, Warwick CV34 5WE, England
Tel. 01926 499 619
Email: info@helion.co.uk Website: www.helion.co.uk Twitter: @helionbooks Visit our blog http://blog.helion.co.uk/

Published by Helion & Company 2023
Designed and typeset by Farr out Publications, Wokingham, Berkshire
Cover designed by Paul Hewitt, Battlefield Design (www.battlefield-design.co.uk)

ISBN 978-1-804513-71-2

British Library Cataloguing-in-Publication Data.
A catalogue record for this book is available from the British Library.

For details of other military history titles published by Helion & Company Limited contact the above address, or visit our website: http://www.helion.co.uk. We always welcome receiving book proposals from prospective authors.

INTRODUCTION

This book is not a novel, although all the characters that will appear and all the events that will be related could well have come from several stories which confirms that reality always surpasses fantasy. This book is not a work of fiction either, but a historical work that started in the most unexpected way, which in turn, confirms it is the research that chooses the authors and not the other way around.

On 17 July 2014, a Malaysia Airlines Boeing 777 commercial plane on a direct flight from Amsterdam to Kuala Lumpur, was shot down over Ukraine, 40km from the Russian border, by a Russian-made anti-aircraft missile. The episode caused the death of all occupants of the aircraft which fell, disintegrated on the town of Hrabove. This generated an international crisis between Russia, Ukraine, the United States and the European Union for the criminal and political responsibilities inherent in the unjustified murder of 298 innocent civilians.

This book began with that takedown. As soon as he became aware of what had happened, the editor of the Argentine newspapers *Los Andes* and *UNO de Mendoza* contacted me in an attempt to obtain more details regarding the hypotheses surrounding the destruction of the Malaysian plane. To their disappointment, I had to tell them that it was inconvenient from a journalistic point of view and unprofessional from a technical point of view, to theorise about the causes of an aircraft accident without any elements of analysis in sight, so I excused myself from commenting. Although all that ended in nothing, the shooting down over Ukraine awakened a distant memory in me, dormant since my adolescence, the vague reference to an Argentine plane that had also been shot down by the Russians in equally confusing circumstances. To specify that episode, I turned to the source of my memory, the book Aviación Comercial Argentina (1945–1980) by Pablo Luciano Potenze, which I had read for the first time in 1987. There, on page 245, in the section corresponding to the Transport company Aéreo Rioplatense, I found the brief reference I had retained in my memory, according to which:

> In July 1981, TAR made the front page of world newspapers when one of its planes crashed in the Soviet Union, making public the transport of arms that the company carried out between Israel and Iran.

The reference to an accident immediately referred me to a regular source of consultation, the Information Bulletins published annually by the Civil Aviation Accident Investigation Board (JIAAC), which in 1981, depended on the Air Regions Command of the Argentine Air Force. I did not find anything there, nor did I find any reference in the pages of specialised Argentine aeronautical publications of the time, specifically the punctilious Aero Mundial (edited by Alberto Mirkin) and the robust Aeroespacio (edited by the Argentine Air Force). This in itself was strange enough, but it became downright suspicious when, on successive trips to Buenos Aires, I found nothing in the official files of the JIAAC, nor in the files of the Undersecretariat of Commercial Air Transport (successor to the National Directorate of Commercial Air Transport of 1981), nor in the files of the National Civil Aviation Administration (successor of the Air Regions Command from 2007). Finally, and to my surprise, I did not find anything in the always orderly Directorate of Historical Studies of the Argentine Air Force or in the always fertile National Aeronautics Library (also dependent on the Air Force).

For an obsessive researcher there is nothing worse than elusive information and I must confess, in the first days of searching, the research object itself seemed to elude me, which ultimately strengthened my tenacity in tracking it down since it was evident that there was something strange surrounding the downing of the Argentine plane. I then decided to search primary sources and I ended up in the newspaper archive of the Los Andes newspaper, which has digitised all its copies from 1882 to date. This formidable computer search engine allowed me to remove the first veil, contextualise the dates and activate a more precise parallel search in La Nación, La Prensa and other periodicals of the time, whose pages I photographed with a digital camera in the newspaper library of the General San Martín Public Library (Mendoza, Argentina). Once this information was processed, I had a firm base from which to project myself onto the internet, which ended up being a really valuable source as it allowed me access to various official publications and sources, including declassified documents from the United States Central Intelligence Agency.

Thanks to the kindness of Drs. Hernán Adrián Gómez and Diego Sebastián Idiart (Director of Air Transport and Head of the National Aircraft Registry Department of the National Civil Aviation Administration, respectively) in 2015, I accessed the technical file of the Canadair CL-44 aircraft registration LV-JTN and, in this way, to the report prepared by the Civil Aviation Accident Investigation Board, a document that otherwise would have been impossible to find since it was never published (which explained why I had not found it in my searches and added even more mystery to the case). With all this new, extremely precise information, I went to the Archives of the Ministry of Foreign Affairs and Worship of the Nation, where I was able to review hundreds of diplomatic communications sent regarding the disappearance of the Argentine freighter.

While the investigation was going on, and at a time when the mosaic of data seemed as if it could never be completed, new official documents hitherto unknown unexpectedly came to light and all from a fortuitous discovery. On 31 October 2013, while maintenance tasks were being carried out in the basement of the Condor Building, headquarters of the Commander-in-Chief of the Argentine Air Force, secret files were unearthed which belonged to the National Reorganisation Process, the military dictatorship that ruled the country between 1976 and 1983. The Air Force decided to communicate the discovery so that it became public, and thus the documents were identified and classified, among which there were several related to Transporte Aéreo Rioplatense.

As a result, I agreed to the charter agreement signed on 7 July 1981 between the company and Stuart McCafferty; and to a confidential memorandum addressed on 30 July 1981 to the Air Force Chief-of-Staff by the then National Director of Commercial Air Transport. These documents, added to those found in the Foreign Ministry Archive, were decisive in confirming the hypothesis of the cover-up perpetrated by the Argentine State regarding the demolition of the Canadair CL-44 of TAR. The cover-up carried out by the Union of Soviet Socialist Republics was much more difficult to elucidate, largely because the USSR had been dissolved since 1991, so it no longer existed as a state at the time this investigation began. However, little by little, I managed to lift the veil based on the statements of Valentin Kulyapin, the Russian pilot who had shot down the Argentine plane, who still lives in Moscow and claims the right to be considered a Hero of Russia for the actions he carried out on 18 July 1981 in the skies of Armenia. Kulyapin had been severely questioned by Colonel Marat Syrtlanov, whose effort to expose the fraud surrounding the downing of the Argentine plane not only shed light on the Soviet cover-up, but also showed me that there are still decent people in the world for whom the truth constitutes a value to defend. It goes without saying, that the correspondence with Colonel Syrtlanov was particularly fruitful for me.

At one point, in the middle of the investigation, I got completely bogged down by conflicting accounts, false data and maliciously misrepresented information. At that moment (which was not a single moment, but a period) I decided to archive everything and forget about it, because it seemed impossible to find a meaning or a thread to the events. However, one afternoon, I found myself looking in silence at the documentation libraries that I had accumulated so far and, in order not to waste the time invested, I decided to start over. This was literal, because I deleted everything I had written and started again, from scratch. Since I already knew that the available information was full of pitfalls, I went slowly, taking nothing for granted and citing the source of every relevant piece of information, no matter how small. Little by little, a first layer of solid information emerged, below which the others gradually appeared. Then, unexpectedly, the whole story popped into my head as a logical whole and I could not stop writing. The references that I took as notes are today the bibliographical citations that show where the information came from to write each chapter.

The first draft of this book was finished on 15 December 2018 in the format presented today. As usually happens in complex investigations, at no time was there a single line of argument, but several moving in parallel, which made the job really difficult, especially when I noticed the succession of official cover-ups that had surrounded each of the episodes in Israel, Iran, the United States, Argentina and the Soviet Union. That being the case, I worked on each axis separately and only at the end, when assembling them, was I able to have the overall vision that is presented today as a complete work.

Although this book was written under the protection of my aeronautical library, the research and writing was carried out without physical anchoring, separately polishing parts initially disconnected from each other. By way of example, it is enough to indicate that the general plan of the work was drawn up on the morning of 14 October 2014, at some point between Mendoza and Buenos Aires, while I was occupying seat 14A of the Airbus A320 on the LAN 4253 flight. The title arose at 9:30 p.m. of the same day, on the return flight, LAN 4252.

One of the main obstacles that this investigation went through was the language. A large part of events covered in this book had their epicentre between the Middle East and the Far East, in the territories that we know today as Russia, Israel, Armenia and Iran. That would not be too relevant, if it were not for the fact that each of these countries is home to different cultures who have a different language and a different way of writing. By way of example, the word Armenia is spelled Армения in Russian, הינמרא in Hebrew, ناتسنمرا in Persian, and Հայաստան in Armenian. (Additionally, Cyrillic and Armenian characters are written from left to right, while Hebrew and Persian are written from right to left). Searching for and understanding information about the disappearance of the Argentine plane in documents or computer portals written in these languages was a head start, which more than once led me to think that the biblical account of the tower of Babel (erected precisely in those latitudes), because if God intended to confuse and disperse men based on their differences in language, he really did it with great success. What struck me the most was that, in addition to the spelling differences, there is also a notable difference in pronunciation. If we pronounce the word Armenia while in Armenia, it is very likely that a local does not understand what we are saying at all.

Another obstacle was related to the computation of time. In Argentina and generally throughout the West, we take for granted that the days of the week go from Monday to Sunday, that the months of the year go from January to December and that the years are counted from the birth of Jesus. But all these parameters correspond to the Gregorian calendar, in force in the Christian world from 1582, when Pope Gregory XIII instituted it. In the Hebrew, Persian and Muslim calendars, the parameters are different, all official and of obligatory application in their respective territories or spheres of cultural influence. Thus, on Saturday 18 July 1981, the date on which the Canadair CL-44 of Transporte Aéreo Rioplatense disappeared according to the Western calendar in force in Buenos Aires, it was 27 Tir 1360 in Tehran, and 16 Ramadan 1401 in Ankara. and on 16 Tamuz 5741 in Tel Aviv – just to mention the capitals of three of the countries where the events reported in this book took place.

While the Gregorian calendar starts from the birth of Jesus, the Muslim calendar begins from the year in which the Prophet Muhammad began his pilgrimage from Mecca to Medina (Hegira), while the Hebrew calendar begins with the departure of the Jews from Egypt (Exodus). Additionally, the non-working day of the week changes according to each culture, since the inactivity of Western Sunday corresponds to Saturday in Jewish culture and Friday in the Muslim world. To confuse matters further, in the Hebrew and Muslim calendars, the day does not begin with sunrise, but with sunset. All these differences became a problem when it came to pinpointing exact dates according to the Western calendar and for the historical purposes of this book. The determination of hours was also torture, due to the difference in time zones around the planet. Suffice it to point out that in Tehran, the easternmost city in this story, clocks are seven and a half hours 'advanced' with respect to Buenos Aires, simply because the sun rises there seven and a half hours earlier. Thus, 9:00 p.m. on a Sunday in Argentina (last day of our week) corresponds to 4:30 a.m. on a do-shanbeh in Iran (third day of the Persian week). It is therefore inevitable that in the course of this work, some error has occurred in the calculation of the schedules, although the dates cited are precise, since they were calculated and confirmed on repeated occasions.

A job of this magnitude would not have been possible without the collaboration of many people. The first of these was my wife, Carina Cocuelle, whose daily support allowed me to have the necessary time to carry out the investigation. The many hours that this book demanded, throughout almost five years, were hours of absence for my family, so it was my wife who had to bear most of the housework and raising our daughter, Mercedes. I hope that by seeing this finished book you can both understand what I was doing on so many nights late for dinner or ending up in bed until the small hours of the morning.

All historical research is, in reality, a collective work, since an author is always based on the works, references and background of other historians. In my case, at all times I felt that I was standing on the shoulders of titans, for which I want to thank the aeronautical researchers Francisco Halbritter, Marcelo W. Miranda, Guido Ghiretti, Pablo Potenze, Gabriel Tomás Pavlovcic, Esteban Raczynski, Michael Magnusson, Luis Alberto Franco, Oscar Bellini, Atilio Baldini, Peter Amos, Alan Brough, Mikhail D. Guskov, Malcolm Porter and Bob Ruffle, many of them longtime members of Air Britain Historians. My thanks also to all those who made photographic material available to me, whose names appear in the credits of each photo published in this book.

Particularly useful was the collaboration of pilots from the extinct companies Aerotransportes Entre Ríos and Transporte Aéreo Rioplatense, especially Juan Neto and Héctor Montioli. The drafts of this book were reviewed by the pilots Pablo Mousten, Héctor Biondini and Raúl Conti, whose experience in the mentioned cargoes was particularly useful for correcting the original text.

My thanks also go to Agustina Saubidet, Palmira and Carlos FitzGerald, for sharing the memories and photos of another TAR pilot, the well-remembered Miguel Lawler FitzGerald. I would like to express particular appreciation to Oscar Palacio, in charge of live cargo in that company, for the richness of his testimonies and for sharing graphic and documentary material treasured over decades in memory of the crew members who died on the Canadair CL-44 that motivated this book. In the same sense, I cannot fail to mention Roberto Melo, a Uruguayan aeronautical technician, who served in the AER and TAR freighters, since his memories shed particular light on the most sensitive aspects of this story. It is an honour for me that both Oscar Palacio and Roberto Melo have agreed to collaborate on this book, since they are the last two living witnesses of those flights to Iran that ended in tragedy.

One of the biggest difficulties I encountered during the research was accessing sources written in the Russian, Persian and Hebrew languages, whose characters and scripts were truly unintelligible to me. I would therefore like to thank my English teacher, Guadalupe Campoy, who put me in contact with the Russian translator Miguel Borisov, with whose help I was able to unravel texts that had been inaccessible up to now. My thanks also go to Fabián Corzo, a good friend who is also a polyglot.

A special mention deserves the plastic artist Christian Zambruno, who drew all the illustrations in this book. The quality of his profiles and his drawings constitutes one of the best gifts that could be given to a reader.

In all the organisations that I went to, I found warmth and a positive response. I wish to express my gratitude to Estela Balzi (National Library of Aeronautics), Julia Scarensi (Archive of the Ministry of Foreign Relations and Worship), Dr. Cecilia Susana Fernández (Director of Legal Affairs of the Civil Aviation Accident Investigation Board), Commodore (RE) Oscar Luis Aranda Durañona (Director of Historical Studies of the Argentine Air Force), Karina Derderian and Professor Sergio Kniasian (Armenian Centre of the Argentine Republic), and Professor Cecilia García Novarini (Equipment Coordinator of Work of the Program for the Modernisation of Archives of the Armed Forces).

Gustavo Marón

Las Compuertas, Luján de Cuyo, Mendoza, Argentina

9th December 2022

1

THE WORLD BELONGS TO THE DARING

Each of the segments that make up the history of Argentine Civil Aviation is full of personalities, anecdotes and surprises. It is enough to pay attention, investigate a little and to be stunned, since our country has generated countless entrepreneurs who, at the same time, have undergone truly legendary ventures. This is the case of the two companies that motivated this book, by far the largest freighters in Argentina and at the time, also the most important in Latin America. Although they were born in succession, both ended up operating together, so had a common ending. It is time to remember them, so that their imprint and legacy are not lost in the sands of time.

Edgardo Luzzi, founding father of Aerotransportes Entre Ríos, seen inside Compartment B of one of his company's three Canadair Yukons. Through talent, tenacity and future vision, he built a transportation empire from scratch. (Héctor Biondini)

Aerotransportes Entre Ríos was born from the implosion of Transcontinental, a company founded in 1957 with the purpose of satisfying the demands for air transport from the private sector that were not being properly met by the state company Aerolíneas Argentinas. Transcontinental alone is well worth a book, because it constituted a true entrepreneurship that left a deep legacy, but here I will only say that it ended very badly, in a call for bankruptcy at the end of 1961, with a twin-engine Curtiss C-46 Commando and two four-engined Bristol Britannias being repossessed by the Industrial Bank.

As it could not be otherwise, all Transcontinental personnel were separated from the company as a result of the bankruptcy. Generally, they were absorbed by the other airlines that continued to operate, especially Aerolíneas Argentinas, which could never be merged as it was a state company, a characteristic that, paradoxically, had been one of the causes of the TSA implosion. Aerolíneas had been competing in the market in unequal conditions since, as a state company, it could never go bankrupt. Its chronic deficit was (and would be in the future) covered by contributions from the treasury, generating unfair competition for genuinely private companies (and genuine companies).[1]

Those unemployed due to the bankruptcy of Transcontinental and who were not absorbed by Aerolíneas Argentinas or other airlines, ended up going from hangar to hangar, asking for work with the anguish and despair of those who have no way to support their families. Among them was the aeronautical technician, Edgardo Luzzi and the line pilots Ernesto Wood and Emilio González Bonorino, three friends who wore out their shoes between Ezeiza airport and Aeroparque, while crying out to God for help.

It seems that God listened to them and he sent them a golden opportunity that literally fell from heaven. On 28 January 1962, about 10km southwest of Paso Grande, San Luis province, a twin-engine Curtiss C-46 Commando smuggler with Uruguayan registration, crash landed. It was the C-46A-55-CK registered CX-AYI, owned by Juan Adorisio and the remains of the aircraft were preserved in the hope of being recovered. However, the damage was so extensive the owner claimed the insurance and declared the plane lost, but the hull was left in the hands of La Universal Compañía Argentina de Seguros S.A. The insurance company tried to recover part of the

Technicians pose next to two Curtiss C-46 (CW-20T) from the company Transcontinental, one of several large private airlines of Argentina at the time. All of them would be fired in late 1961 as a result of summons from creditors that would end in the bankruptcy for the company. Seventh from left is Edgard Luzzi. (Edgardo Luzzi)

cost by fixing and putting the plane up for sale and for this purpose it summoned aeronautical technician Edgardo Luzzi.[2]

When the old mechanic came across the wrecked freighter in the middle of the beautiful San Luis landscape, his pupils dilated with enthusiasm as it was an airplane of the same type and model as the C-46 interdicted in the bankruptcy of Transcontinental but with a wide cargo door on the left side. This meant that the Transcontinental plane could be transformed from parts from its smuggler twin, which could in turn be cannibalised to provide two spare engines, spare parts, cockpit instrumentation and other critical components.

Luzzi returned from San Luis with a burning soul and he saw the possibility of establishing his own cargo company with his friends. The three knew the enormous gap in the market that was neglected by the air transport companies operating in the country, starting with Aerolíneas Argentinas, which considered cargo something dirty and unworthy. However, there was a future in cargo as the country and the world were expanding and there was an oversupply of freighter planes (or convertibles to freighters). In cargo transportation, hundreds of passengers are replaced by a single person – the customer – who tended to be very satisfied if the merchandise was delivered on time and he would inevitably renew the contract or recommend the cargo company.

Thus, the three unemployed launched into forming their own company without a single penny. Undoubtedly, they had plenty of attitude and determination, although they also had a share of luck as Ernesto Wood was a personal friend of the owner of La Universal. This being the case, he proposed to buy the plane that crashed in

C-46A registration LV-PCU (the future LV-FTO) of Transcontinental S. A., a twin of the LV-FTR that was rescued by Edgardo Luzzi from bankruptcy and converted into the first freighter of Aerotransportes Entre Ríos S. R. L. (Guido Ghiretti)

San Luis, in the condition and in the place where it was located, at an auction price and in payable six monthly instalments. The insurer accepted – otherwise they would have recovered no costs at all – and the three friends looked set to acquire a fabled freighter.

As soon as the purchase of the damaged freighter was agreed, Edgardo Luzzi appeared before the Transcontinental bankruptcy judge and requested the assignment of the Curtiss C-46 Commando in the judicial process. It was the C-46A-41-CU registration LV-FTR, transformed into a civil version CW-20T, which Luzzi proposed to convert into a freighter, put it to fly and pay for it with the proceeds of his work. The judge, probably moved by the mechanic's determination and audacity, granted the request. What followed was a frantic race to recover the crashed sister plane in San Luis, as the three friends were not willing to pass up the opportunity that Providence had offered them.

The C-46 smuggler was transferred to the San Luis town of La Toma, where the reinforced floor and the section of the fuselage where the cargo door was located were removed. These parts were sent to Ezeiza together with the engines, the half wings, the gear landing gear, tail drifts and rudders and all other pieces or parts that could be removed. The work was of such magnitude that to complete it in the short time available, Luzzi summoned another good friend of his, the aeronautical technician Enrique Pascual Tomassini, to whom he proposed to become the fourth shareholder of the cargo company that he was about to form.

Thus, with two pilots and two mechanics as owners, AER was born in April 1962, whose name was as whimsical as the vicissitudes of its own origin; it was named in honour of the homonymous Mesopotamian province, whose government had promised the founders a credit for the constitution that was never granted.

On 12 September 1962, through Provision No. 215/62 of the National Directorate of Aero-Commercial Transport, the company was authorised to provide non-regular internal cargo services for a term of three years, with its 'brand new' C- 46F. Barely four months later, on 28 January 1963, it was also authorised to make non-scheduled international flights with the same plane. AER then opened a modest administrative and commercial office on the third floor of Calle Tucumán 1441, Capital Federal and set up a maintenance workshop at the Ezeiza International Airport, headed by Edgardo Luzzi. Carrying out their own maintenance was one of the greatest successes of the company whose solitary C-46 was soon discovered flying to Mexico, Uruguay, Panama, Chile, Peru, Venezuela and the United States, the vast majority of the times with loads of cattle standing.[3]

With the Curtiss C-46 always operating at maximum capacity, Aerotransportes Entre Ríos was immediately profitable, thus generating the necessary profits to pay for the plane in the bankruptcy of Transcontinental and in addition, to buy two other planes. Specifically, these were the four-engine long-range Lockheed L-749 Constellation registration LV-IGS (purchased on 5 March 1964 from the Dutch flag carrier KLM) and the small twin-engined Beechcraft C-45F Expeditor registration LV-GTA, which was purchased on 3 March 1966 to James Puig, who used it to transfer small loads in short trips. The company's growth was so explosive

Edgardo Luzzi (first from left) with the smuggler C-46 registration CX-AYI that crashed on 28 January 1962, in San Luis province, Argentina. Notable is the damage to the nose. (Edgardo Luzzi via Esteban Raczynski)

The remains of the smuggler C-46 registration CX-AXI, which crashed in San Luis on 28 February 1962, seen after being cannibalised by Edgardo Luzzi. Notable is the hole in the fuselage left when the cargo door was removed; this was necessary to convert the Transcontinental LV-FTR into a freighter. (Frederico Kirbus)

The C-46 (i.e., CW-20T) registration LV-FTR after being converted into a freighter by Edgardo Luzzi, with the colours and titles of Aerotransportes Entre Ríos, the company he formed together with Ernesto Wood and Emilio González Bonorino. The photograph was taken at Ezeiza, on 22 July 1964. (Marcelo W. Miranda)

The Lockheed L-749 Constellation with registration LV-IGS, the first four-engined aircraft purchased by Aerotransportes Entre Ríos, seen at Gatwick International, outside London, on 10 September 1966. (Alan Bus)

that the managers crowded into the small office on Calle Tucumán soon moved to Montevideo 125, second floor, finally ending up in the comfortable building at Leandro N. Alem 639.

With three freighters that complemented each other and the winning charisma typical of its founding partners, Aerotransportes Entre Ríos began to expand in the niche market that Aerolíneas Argentinas had despised so much, competing with several other national companies that also operated Curtiss C-46, among them being Austral, Aerovías Halcón and Transamerican Air Transport.

Little by little, with effort and talent, AER forged ahead and it soon became clear that it would need more aircraft in its fleet. In search of planes, at the beginning of 1967 Ernesto Wood travelled to Miami whose international airport was already one of the most important nodes in the world, since it captured practically all the air traffic that moved to and from Central America, the Caribbean and South America This also meant that much of the international market for used transport aircraft was catalysed there. Once in Miami, Wood made contact with George Edward Batchelor, a character as talented and daring as the Argentine entrepreneurs themselves, whose biographical reference is fundamental in this work as it would also be decisive in the history of Transporte Aéreo Rioplatense.

George Batchelor was born in Shawnee, Oklahoma, on 20 December 1920, and began flying in 1936 when he was just 16 years old. Four years later, in 1940, he graduated in Aeronautical Engineering from the Aeronautical Institute of California, from which time he began working at the Bell Aircraft Corporation factories (assisting in the design of the P-39 Airacobra fighter) and North American Aviation (in the P-51 Mustang fighter design office). When the United States entered the Second World War after the Japanese attack on Pearl Harbour on 7 December 1941, Batchelor enlisted in the US Army Air Corps, where he achieved the rank of major. It was precisely during his military service, repeatedly flying cargo planes between the United States and Europe, that Batchelor began to envision his future as an air transport entrepreneur.

After the war ended in 1945 and with vast experience operating heavy freighters, especially Douglas DC-4s, Batchelor began flying as a pilot for National Airlines, one of the largest air transport companies in the United States. In 1946 it had moved its base of operations to the Miami International Airport, from where it flew regularly to Havana (Cuba) and New York. The experience gained at National allowed Batchelor to dream of his own company and in 1947, he formed Arrow Airlines Incorporated, a company that he hoped would engage in tourist and cargo flights. To capitalise on this, he bought at auction, a Douglas DC-3, left over from the war, which was demobilised at an air base in Hawaii.

Since the plane did not have enough range to make a direct flight to California, Batchelor crossed to Hawaii, modified the original fuel system with a homemade overhaul and crossed the Pacific to the United States with supplemental fuel tanks. Arriving in Santa Monica, California, he sold the plane for $25,000 and injected that capital into the newly formed Arrow Airlines, which was formally incorporated on 12 August 1949. To give an idea of the company's humble origins and Batchelor's ambition, it is enough to highlight that the operations office was built with wooden boxes (previously used to store engines) on the small landing strip of Lomita (future Municipal Airport of Torrance).

Arrow Airlines began with a great tragedy as on 7 December 1949, it lost its Douglas DC-3 registration N60256 over the hills of Benicia, California. Among the passengers who died were Lorraine B. Batchelor (26 years old) and her baby Patrick (2 years old), the wife and son of George Batchelor. The blow was tremendous for the founder of the company but it did not deter him in his efforts to succeed and by 1952, Arrow Airlines was once again established as one of the most important, non-scheduled carriers in the interior of California. However, in 1954, the Civil Aviation Board (predecessor of the Federal Aviation Administration) suspended the company's non-scheduled air transport certificate for detecting that it was making more charter flights between Los Angeles and New York than it was allowed. With this background and realising that the new federal air transport regulations would make competition very difficult in the future, Batchelor began to diversify his aeronautical businesses.

With a business vision worthy of a pioneer, Batchelor concentrated the air operations of Arrow Airlines in the air cargo segment and in 1964, moved the operational base to Miami, which at that time was becoming a true catalyst for air transport generated in Latin America. The same year he founded an aircraft rental company (International Aerodyne) plus a supplier of spare parts (Interair Parts), both followed in 1965 by a used aircraft sales company (International Air Leases), a front company for triangulations (Liberty Air), a maintenance workshop (Batch-Air) and the financial company that would allow oiling the operations of all the companies (Aero Finance Incorporated).[4]

In 1967, upon meeting Ernesto Wood in Miami and becoming aware of the existence and potential of Aerotransportes Entre Ríos, George Batchelor decided to strengthen the company and he agreed to lease their planes. Thus, AER experienced an impressive leap, incorporating between 1967 and 1968 four Lockheed L-1049H Super Constellation freighters (registered LV-IXZ, LV-JHF, LV-JIO and LV-JJO), all leased to Aerodyne, which was the company owned by Batchelor. In 1969, a new aircraft was incorporated (the eighth of its fleet), which turned out to be the heavy freighter Bristol Britannia registered LV-JNL, leased to Batch-Air, another firm belonging to the North American multi-businessman.

With all these aircraft in service, Aerotransportes Entre Ríos took the lead over all its competitors and virtually monopolised several international cargo segments, including live cargo transportation. To give an idea of the volume, it is enough to indicate that, in 1969 alone, the company transported 717 horses, 1,788 cows, 997 sheep, 76 pigs, eight dogs, six monkeys, two tigers and two lions. In this context of growth, Ernesto Wood fell seriously ill and decided to retire from the company. So also did Emilio González Bonorino but chose to devote himself to politics (in 1973 he would become Minister of Economy of the Province of Mendoza, during the Peronist government of Dr. Alberto Martínez Baca).

Roberto Otto Lucas, one of the last shareholders of Aerotransportes Entre Ríos, in the cabin of a Canadair Yukon belonging to the company. He was part of an elite group of legendary cargo commanders for whom the word 'impossible' did not exist. (Héctor Biondini)

Faced with this situation, on 13 August 1969, Edgardo Luzzi and Tomassini entered into an agreement with George Batchelor to capitalise the company, selling him 25 percent of the shares (those that were formally registered in the name of González Bonorino). The company was legally transformed from a limited liability company (SRL) to a public limited company (SA), incorporating Ricardo María Oliver, Alberto Raúl Mauriño, Rodolfo Alfredo Gordillo, Roberto Otto Lucas, Rodolfo Petrini and Pedro Tomás Alonso as new partners. One of the new shareholders, retired Commodore Jorge Tomás Braceras Hurtado, was appointed president given his good relations with the Argentine Air Force –until 1968 he had served as president of the Air Transport Advisory Board (JATA).[5]

The best aircraft of the thriving and capitalised Aerotransportes Entre Ríos and the one that proved to be the most profitable given its ability to cover long distances with large volumes of cargo, turned out to be the Bristol Britannia, however, its life in the company was extremely short. On 12 July 1970, it was destroyed in a plane accident that occurred at the Ezeiza Airport when its pilot decided to land in adverse weather conditions. The loss of the Britannia was a bitter pill for the owners of AER just at a time when the company was reorganising to expand but it also provided an incentive to quickly produce its replacement, otherwise they risked losing the long-distance market they had so painstakingly achieved. Thus, everyone began to look for a replacement Britannia, since the incorporation of an identical aircraft to the damaged one saved costs in training and maintenance since the company had already trained the crews and even set up a complete workshop.

In September 1970, some friends of Enrique Pascual Tomassini who worked at the Argentine embassy in Caracas, informed him that the Canadian government had put up for sale the 12 Canadair CC-106 Yukons that had made up the squadrons of transport 437 and 412 of the Royal Canadian Air Force. It was offering them to all the countries with which Canada had diplomatic relations. These were aircraft substantially similar to the Britannia, as they had been developed by Canadair Limited from its blueprints, albeit with Rolls-Royce Tyne turboprop engines instead of the original Bristol Proteus. In jargon, they were simply known as the 'Canadian Britannia'.

George Edward Batchelor, an American businessman, was a key figure in the development of Aerotransportes Entre Ríos and later, of Transportes Aéreo Rioplatense. (USA Today)

Tomassini immediately brought the news to the attention of his partners since there was the possibility of getting a plane at a discount price. However, shortly after finding out, it turned out that the Canadians did not sell the Yukons individually but in batches, with all their spare parts, ground equipment and extra engines. It was a fantastic opportunity to get excellent aircraft in sufficient numbers and condition to make Aerotransportes Entre Ríos the largest cargo company in the world, however, the company's capital simply was not large enough. A that point, George Batchelor entered the scene, a man not willing to miss the opportunity despite the fact that he had his focus elsewhere – it was precisely at the moment he was negotiating the purchase of the airline Capitol International Airways.

Batchelor proposed to Edgardo Luzzi that he take charge of the entire Canadian complete package purchase, for whose financing he would interest New York investors gathered around the companies Aerodyne, Beaver Enterprises and Compañía Interamericana Export-Import-Brokerage Co. In exchange and as compensation for his actions, Batchelor promised to deliver to Aerotransportes Entre Ríos, financed and at cost price, four Canadair CC-106 Yukons. For the Argentines it was an incredible boost and for North American investors, it ended up being a heavenly business, as they paid USD 365,000 per plane to later sell it for USD 1,200,000. The biggest beneficiary was George Batchelor who kept the entire stock of spare parts and extra engines, with which he capitalised on his aeronautical shop, Batch-Air. In the following years, this company would become very rich with the sale of spare parts and the maintenance service provided not only to the 12 CC-106s, but also to the 27 civilian CL-44s that Canadair Limited had been building in parallel.[6]

Of the four CC-106 Yukons committed by George Batchelor, Aerotransportes Entre Ríos only decided to incorporate three into its fleet. The fourth aircraft, which also received Argentine registration, was actually used as a legal springboard to introduce the model in Peru. Indeed, the Peruvian aeronautical authorities did not admit the certification and subsequent civil registration of an aircraft that had originally been military, while the Aeronautical Certifications Department of the Argentine National Airworthiness Directorate did allow this as the CC-106 was nothing other than the military version of the civil model CL-44, which was certified as such by the Canadian Department of Transport and the North American Federal Aviation Administration. Thus, AER's fourth Yukon was certified and registered in Argentina (as LV-JZR) and later sold to Aeronaves del Perú, which registered it OB-R-1005.

The first CC-106 Yukon of Aerotransportes Entre Ríos was registered LV-JSY, which Batch-Air offered for rent with the option to buy (leasing) on 13 November 1970. It was received at the Saskatoon International Airport, Saskatchewan, by Roberto Otto Lucas and Edgardo Luzzi, who travelled to Canada to receive simulator and aircraft maintenance training courses, respectively. The second Yukon leased was registered LV-JYR (received November 1971) and the third was LV-LBS (received August 1972). With this addition, the old and faithful Lockheed Super Constellation LV-JIO and LV-JJO were returned to the broker, Aerodyne, who ended up cannibalising them to serve as spare stowages. AER kept only one operational Connie, the L-749 Constellation registered LV-IGS, since the LV-IXZ had been broken in April 1970 during a repair in Ezeiza, when the plane fell on one of the jacks that supported it, damaging one of the wings.

Aerotransportes Entre Ríos was the first civilian operator of the Canadair CC-106 Yukon and one of those who used it the most. Unfortunately, the good fortune that had accompanied the company from the very moment of its constitution, ran out on 20 July 1972, when the LV-JYR crashed into Cerro Aconcagua, Mendoza, while transporting 89 cows from Montevideo to Santiago de Chile. The blow was devastating for the entire family that made up the company, since six crew members died in the episode. Three years later, on 27 September 1975, another six lives would be lost when LV-JSY crashed while trying to take off from runway 27L at Miami International Airport.[7]

At that time, the company entered into a deep economic and emotional crisis. However, what emerged in the most unlikely way, was two of its pilots, Carlos Martínez Guerrero and Armando Tola, had separated to form their own company Transporte Aéreo Rioplatense (TAR), which in turn, would have to recover and redirect the destinies of their predecessor.

2

THE RISE OF TAR

Carlos Martínez Guerrero was an exceptional aviator and a man with a head for business. He had started his aeronautical life at the age of 20 in 1942 and two years later, he received a scholarship from the North American government to take a professional pilot course at Randolph Field, Texas, home of the United States Army Air Forces Central Instructors School, from which he graduated with his Flight Instructor certification. With this background, he returned to Argentina and began to work in the General Directorate of Civil Aeronautics which assigned him as an instructor at the Aero Club La Plata.

In 1946, Martínez Guerrero began working in the mixed economy company, Aeroposta Argentina (Aerolíneas Argentinas from 1950) and later, in the private companies Transcontinental, Austral Líneas Aéreas and finally, Aerotransportes Entre Ríos, where he took a liking to international cargo. In these ventures, he flew all manner of heavy aircraft, from Second World War surplus Curtiss C-46 Commando twin-engines to post-war four-engine Lockheed L-1049H Super Constellation and Bristol Britannia builds. One and then the other revealed the secrets of the cargo market and through each one he discovered new business opportunities. He thus came to the conclusion that there were fabulous opportunities for a drop-tail freighter like the Canadair CL-44D Swingtail, with which he could transport all the bulky goods that could not fit into the holds of Aerotransportes Entre Ríos planes.[1]

Determined to form his own company, Martínez Guerrero had the decency to share his business strategy with AER's board members, who in turn, recommended George Batchelor to help him discover the best Swingtail available on the market. Quick as lightning, Batchelor put him in touch with Paul J. Finazzo, executive vice president of Airlift International, a company which had the Swingtail registered N605SA for sale in Miami. When Martínez Guerrero saw it, he was fascinated as he immediately understood the enormous potential of this huge plane. For this reason and without further delay, he promised to buy the plane. In order to honour the purchase, he had some of his own funds and in addition, a contribution from the family of his wife, Gloria Susana González Howard who was part of Mendoza's high society.

Already controlled by Carlos Martínez Guerror, Aerotransportes Entre Ríos sold the Canadair CL-44-6 with registration LV-JZB to Atlantida Linea Aérea Sudamericana (ALAS), a company incorporated in Uruguay. On 3 November 1978, the aircraft was re-registered as CX-BKD. Less than a year later, it was lost while making a heavy landing at the Carrasco airport, outside Montevideo. (El Pais)

With the capital collected, in December 1969, Martínez Guerrero and his great friend Armando Tola resigned as commanders of Aerotransportes Entre Ríos and founded TAR, a public limited company designed to operate regular and non-scheduled pure cargo services. The first president of the company was the founder himself, who was accompanied by Carlos P. Baldesarre, Guillermo Martínez Guerrero, Luis Schanstrom and Tola, as directors. The commercial offices of the company were initially installed at Avenida Leandro Alem N° 884 (1001), Capital Federal, although they would later move to Avenida Leandro Alem 734, first floor.[2, 3]

In June 1970, TAR requested authorisation from the National Directorate of Air Transport (under the Ministry of Works and Public Services of the Nation) to operate non-scheduled national and international cargo services with a Canadair CL-44D Swingtail. Given that the maximum take-off weight of the freighter placed it in the category corresponding to a large aircraft, the TAR request was submitted to the public hearing procedure provided for in article 102 of Law 17,285 (Argentine Aeronautical Code), so that the granting authority could analyse 'the convenience, necessity and general usefulness of the services' that it intended to exploit.[4]

As expected, at the public hearing TAR was opposed by Aerolíneas Argentinas, ALA and Austral, which did not want to share the market with any other competitor, even if that competitor only existed on paper. Aerotransportes Entre Ríos was also formally opposed, for the sole purpose of not creating a precedent of weakness before its competitors, although the creation of TAR had already been agreed upon with its founders. To everyone's surprise, Martínez Guerrero appeared at the hearing accompanied by Dr. Agustín Rodríguez Jurado, a prestigious lawyer specialising in Aeronautical Law who was already an eminence at that time, since he was a professor of this subject at the University of Buenos Aires and author of several investigations focused on air transport. As expected, Rodríguez Jurado crushed all the objections of the already established companies, except the one related to allowing TAR to transport cargo cabotage. In a very well planned strategy to win the favourable vote of Aerolíneas Argentinas, Aerotransportes Entre Ríos proposed that the new company be authorised to operate only outside the borders of the Argentine Republic – this actually opened the doors to the rest of the world. Consequently, on 28 July 1970, the de facto President of the Nation, General Roberto Marcelo Levingston, issued Decree No. 850/70 authorising TAR to provide only non-scheduled international cargo services with Canadair CL-44D Swingtail.[5]

With the authorisation of the Argentine government in hand, Carlos Martínez Guerrero and Armando Tola immediately flew to Miami to finalise the purchase of the Swingtail N605SA. There began a long negotiation process with Charles M. Hughes, administrative vice president of Airlift International, which lasted for a period of five months simply as the Argentines did not have enough money to buy the plane, which at dollar value, was very expensive. In addition to all their savings, which were barely enough to pay for a third of the freighter, the enthusiastic founders of TAR could only show off to the Americans their trajectory as pilots, their honesty and the work they claimed to be able to do with the plane they wanted to buy. However, both were convinced they could pay for Canadair with their own flights, to the point that they agreed to buy the N605AS's twin, the N604AS (serial number 33), from Airlift as soon as the first was cancelled. This tenacity ended up paying off and at the beginning of 1971, Airlift agreed to sell them the plane, plus two replacement Rolls-Royce Tyne turbines, plus a batch of spare parts that represented 25 percent of the total inventory that the North American cargo had.

Since TAR did not have all the money to pay for the plane, it was agreed to enter into a leasing contract from 1 March 1971 with a purchase option to be exercised after three years. The rent was set at $17,000 per month (resulting from flying a minimum of 100 hours per month 'boot to boot' at a rate of $170 per hour) while the price of the plane for the exercise of the purchase option was predefined as $1,000,000. TAR undertook to organise its own maintenance workshop to attend to the services, repairs and general overhauls required by the operation of the CL-44D, while Airlift agreed to provide free technical advice and training during the first year of operation. Accepting all these forecasts, the leasing contract was signed in Miami on 22 January 1971 by Paul J. Finazzo and Carlos Martínez Guerrero.[6]

On 17 February 1971, the National Directorate of Air Transport authorised a group of inspectors from the Aircraft and Technical Department of the Promotion and Qualification Directorate of the Air Regions Command of the Argentine Air Force to be sent to Miami to carry out the registration and technical authorisation

The Canadair CL-44 Swingtail with registration LV-JTN in the full colours of TAR on a taxiway at New York's John F. Kennedy International, in November 1978. (Aris Pappas)

The CL-44 Swingtail with registration LV-JZM (twin of the LV-JTN), as seen on 3 November 1973, with its tail folded to the side, at Salzburg International, in Austria. (Michael Bernhard)

of the plan. This would allow it to be transferred to the country bearing Argentine nationality marks. Once the procedure was completed, on 18 March 1971, the National Aircraft Registry registered the CL-44D serial number 34 in the name of TAR S.A., with the civil registration LV-JTN. On 22 March 1971, the Federal Aviation Administration, through its office at the United States Embassy in Buenos Aires, informed the Air Regions Command of the cancellation of the North American registration N605SA.[7]

The entire process of purchasing and registering the CL-44D Swingtail of TAR, took place in parallel with the incorporation process of the four CC-106 Yukons of Aerotransportes Entre Ríos, the first of which (registered LV-JSY) had been incorporated in November 1970. Thus, two private Argentine companies were ready to monopolise heavy transport in the country, especially live cargo, with respect to which their pilots already had vast experience. The two companies were sponsored from the United States by George Batchelor, who hoped that both would expand as in that way, he could earn money as a shareholder of the first and as a supplier of spare parts for both.

On 10 April 1971, the Canadair Swingtail of TAR, with its brand new paint scheme and freshly painted licence plate LV-JTN, landed at the Ezeiza International Airport with a smiling Tola and Martínez Guerrero at the controls. Taking advantage of the transfer flight to Argentina, the plane brought in its hold, materials and equipment related to oil exploitation, the first shipment of the first charter contract signed by the company, courtesy of George Batchelor. Immediately afterwards, the plane took off fully loaded bound for the United States, carrying breeding bulls to Houston, Texas. Two legends of Argentine Aviation were born. One, that of the pilots turned businessmen, that of the teachers who trained their employees, that of the friends who went out to conquer the world. The other, the legend of the folding tail plane, which caused affection and nostalgia among all those who had seen and operated on it, and even more among those who had never seen or operated on it, as befits any true legend.[8]

Partly due to the need to pay Canadair with the flights it was making and partly because of the enthusiasm that flying their own plane meant for them, Martínez Guerrero and Tola launched themselves aggressively in offering the services of TAR. They first went to potential Argentine clients they had met as former Aerotransportes Entre Ríos pilots, whose demands had not been able to be met due to lack of capacity or storage of that company. Thus began a true frenzy of growth that initially led the LV-JTN to close destinations such as Uruguay, Chile, Bolivia, Brazil, Peru and Colombia. As the commercial wheel began to turn, the plane began to fly more and more frequently to and from points as remote as

Canadair CL-44 Swingtail with registration LV-JZM taking off from Glasgow International, in Scotland 1970. (Charlie Stewart)

Basel (Switzerland), Standset, Heathrow and Gatwick (England), Abidjan (Ivory Coast), Malpensa and Linate (Italy), Mallorca and Madrid (Spain), Prestwick (Scotland), Dublin (Ireland), Frankfurt, Munich and Hamburg (Federal Germany), Beauvais (France), New York and Miami (United States), Malmö (Sweden), Tripoli (Libya), Tel Aviv (Israel), Amman (Jordan) and Riyadh (Saudi Arabia), just to mention the most visited destinations.

The profits generated by these cargo flights not only allowed Tola and Martínez Guerrero to pay in advance the lease signed with Airlift International, but also gave them the opportunity to fulfil the promise that both had made to Charles Hughes and Paul Finazzo, in the sense of buying them a second Swingtail as soon as they finished cancelling the first one. Thus, at the end of 1971, negotiations began for a second contract for the Canadair CL-44D4-6 registration N604SA (serial 33). This was operated for a time, in Argentina with North American registration until finally, on 6 June 1972, it was sold and it was registered in the National Aircraft Registry with the registration LV-JZM in the name of TAR.

One of the sources consulted states that George Batchelor mediated in the purchase of this second plane through his Batch-Air aeronautical workshop, which is not surprising considering that at that time he had the world's largest stock of spare parts for CL-44.[9]

In parallel, also at the end of 1971, TAR went looking for a third freighter, which ended up being the Canadair CL-44-6 Yukon serial number 8, for whose transfer to Argentina the passenger registration LV-PRX was obtained in January 1972. This aircraft had served with 437 Squadron of the Royal Canadian Air Force under military registration 15928 (re-registered 106928 in the Canadian Armed Forces registry) and after being decommissioned, was acquired on 18 November 1971 by Beaver Enterprises (the company of the New York investors summoned by Batchelor) and then by Batchelor himself, who left it parked in Montreal. The plane ended up registered in the name of TAR on 17 January 1972.

As anecdotal data, it should be noted that the LV-JZM had suffered an accident on take-off in Viet Nam while it was operating for Airlift as N604SA, for which reason it 'flew crooked'. It also exhibited many other failures, including the loss of hydraulic fluid due to the tail opening actuator, so abundant it had to be collected by a mechanic with a bucket and then reused – which was prohibited.[10]

With three freighters in service, TAR operations increased steadily. The company went from flying 3,067 hours in 1972 to 3,884 hours in 1973, then climbed to 4,685 hours in 1974 and finally reached 5,856 in 1975. In mathematical terms, this meant that in 1975 the Tola and Martínez Guerrero fleet had remained in continuous flight during 244 of the 365 days of the year. The cargoes transported were some of the strangest and were destined for the most diverse geographical locations in the world: the rudder of a ship from Paramaribo to Dakar, thoroughbred horses from Buenos Aires to Amman, frozen fish from Bahía Blanca to Madrid, oil rigs from Miami to Riyadh, cold meat from Ezeiza to Tripoli or Tunis, malt from Glasgow to Dublin, cars from Mendoza to Arica, hydroelectric turbines from São Paulo to Santo Domingo and even the entire Moscow Circus from Buenos Aires to Madrid.

Although the transfers of heavy machinery were frequent and profitable, the company was characterised by moving live cargo, whose volumes were truly impressive simply due to the storage the Swingtail allowed. In fact, the main hold enabled a 'double' floor to

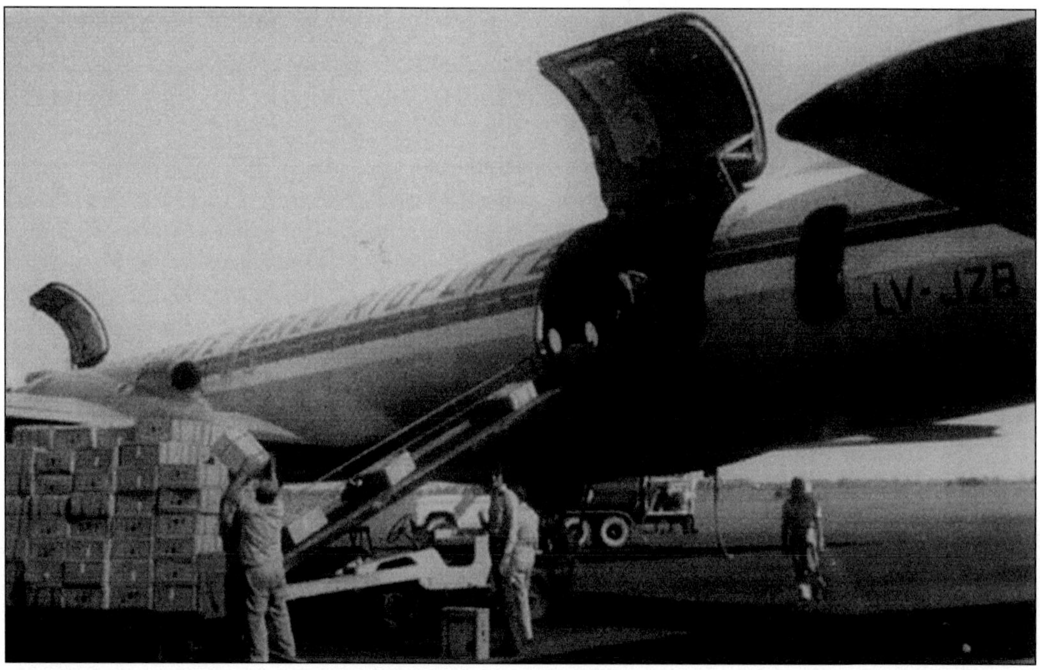

CC-106 Yukon with registration LV-JZB seen loading cargo through its side doors, at Ezeiza International Airport. Notable is the absence of the folding tail mechanism. (Héctor Biondini)

The Bristol 175 Britannia 312F, with registration LV-JNL, the first heavy freighter of Aerotransportes Entre Ríos, photographed at the Aeroparque de la Ciudad de Buenos Aires, in March 1970. (Werner Fischdick)

The Canadair CC-106 Yukon with registration LV-JSY (ex-CAF 106925), at the moment of being delivered to Aerotransportes Entre Ríos at the Canadian airport of Saskatoon, on 12 November 1970. First from left is Edgardo Luzzi, who commissioned George Batchelor to purchase 12 decommissioned transports. (Edgardo Luzzi via Esteban Raczynski)

be built in order to transport small animals, so the load capacity was doubled. Thus, it was very common to carry out transcordilleran or transatlantic flights with 400 calves, 50 pigs, 600 sheep, 30 racehorses, 20 breeding bulls or indeed any animal whose transport by air was economically profitable for the client. Usually, these flights were used to also transport other items as below the cargo bay floor, the CL-44 had a second hold, which at the same time was divided into two (front and rear), where luggage or boxes could be accommodated

Without forgetting the economic importance that the movement of large volumes represented for TAR, it was the special loads that allowed the company to obtain greater revenue. These were products classified as dangerous goods in the nomenclatures that the International Air Transport Association (IATA) had in force, including toxic and non-toxic flammable gases, flammable, explosive and self-reactive liquids and solids, oxidisers, organic peroxides, corrosive materials, hypergolic propellants, poisonous waste, magnetised elements and weaponry. On some occasions, the transport requirements for these goods reached the company directly, but in most cases, it was produced by referral from another cargo that, due to lack of storage or scope of insurance coverage, could not meet the client's demands. This was the case for the British company Transmeridian Air Cargo and the Swiss company Transvalair, which in exchange for a commission, transferred to TAR, those flights that for operational or commercial reasons, they were unable to handle.

While the star of TAR was on the rise, that of Aerotransportes Entre Ríos seemed to not stop falling. On 12 July 1970, at a time when Martínez Guerrero was negotiating the purchase of the Swingtail, AER lost the Bristol Britannia LV-JNL in an accident at Ezeiza Airport. Two years later, 20 on July 1972, when TAR was already operating its third CL-44, AER lost the CC-106 Yukon registered LV-JYR over the Andes mountain range, which crashed into Cerro Aconcagua. Three years later, on 27 September 1975, 'La Entre Ríos' lost the Yukon registered LV-JSY at Miami Airport, while it was taking off empty and bound for Houston where it planned to ship cattle. This accident, the third in five years, was the last straw for the shareholders, who made the decision to sell the company. At that time, the company had only two aircraft in its inventory, the Yukon LV-LBS and LV-JZB, but the first was out of service and the

Edgardo Luzzi (first from left), and two Argentine mechanics at the time of receiving the first Canadair CL-44-6 Yukon for Aerotransportes Entre Ríos. For the ferry flight to Argentina, the aircraft wore the registration LV-PQL and had its Canadian military markings removed. The final registration LV-JSY was applied only after arrival in Argentina. (Edgardo Luzzi via Esteban Raczynski)

The Canadair CL-44-6 with registration LV-JYR (ex-CC-106 15927 and RCAF's number 106927), as seen on its arrival at Ezeiza International, Argentina, in December 1971. Notably, the title of Aerotransportes Entre Ríos was not yet applied, although all the Canadian markings had been erased. Six months later, this aircraft would crash against the Aconcagua mountain. (Marcelo W. Miranda)

second had been leased to TAR since January 1972, so in reality, the capacity of AER was nil.

In this context, the best thing that AER's shareholders could do was to offer their company for sale to TAR's shareholders, and in the end they did so. In the words of Edgardo Luzzi:

> When we decided to sell, we knew that TAR had problems with the engines and propellers of the CL-44. I had studied the market for these planes very well and knew what their Achilles heel was. That is why when we bought ours from Batchelor and had the opportunity to choose the spare parts, we took the opportunity to keep eight engines, four propellers and 12 sets of brakes, which were the only remnants of an airplane that was no longer manufactured. At the end of 1975 we went to Martínez Guerrero with our proposal. We told him that we were going to sell the company and that we knew it needed engines. We offered to sell him the company and parts we had. He accepted and we fixed the price, we made a two-year deal. There was a transition period and on 30 April 1976 we handed over AER.[11]

Being the owner of an incomparable strategic vision, Carlos Martínez Guerrero decided to keep the two companies legally separate as two different commercial companies, although in February 1976, in the last part of the transition process, he linked them through a business cooperation agreement. In this way, each one maintained its individuality and its name in the market, but the two began to work together in a more rational way, with mutual exchange of aircraft, technical assistance and application of uniform rates. Thus, progressively, they ended up conducting all types of transport worldwide, 'competing' with each other with different prices in front of new clients, making a common cause in matters of common interest and watching each other's backs against third-party competitors.

The transfer of AER's share package practically coincided with the beginning of the National Reorganisation Process, the military dictatorship that began to rule Argentina after the coup d'état on 24 March 1976. The atmosphere became thick from many points of view, particularly an economic one, since the national economy had been in a tailspin since 1975. Thus, and without any prospect of immediate improvement, TAR and AER decided to jointly exploit their greatest advantage (charging foreign customers in dollars) and dedicated themselves to flying 'beyond the ocean sea', operating in many cases, without even touching Argentine territory. This was made legally possible by application of the Fifth Freedom of the Air enshrined in the International Civil Aviation Agreement signed in 1944 in Chicago, according to which, a company registered in a state signatory to the treaty, could take and disembark in other countries, passengers, mail or cargo destined for (or coming from) third States.

By virtue of the strategic agreement signed between TAR and Aerotransportes Entre Ríos, both companies agreed to use the maximum of their available warehouses, which meant that each of their planes would always fly full, with the subsequent reduction of direct costs and indirect maintenance of integrated fleets. In parallel, it was agreed to maintain at all times, an equivalent number of freighters in each company, so that both would have identical operational capacity in the event of any of their aircraft being put out of service, mainly for maintenance reasons. In addition, it was agreed to integrate crews, uniform salaries and provide mutual operational support in the different bases that both companies had in the country and abroad. In order to make the integration equitable, during the transition period, a coordination committee was formed made up of the operations and maintenance managers of the two companies and chaired on a rotating basis by a representative of each one.

The strategy promoted by Carlos Martínez Guerrero achieved, from one day to the next, that TAR and AER rationally divided the market, preserved employment sources and were mutually protected from third parties. The results were extraordinary. By 1977, the agreement formed by TAR and AER was one of the largest Canadair CL-44 operators in the world, above TRAMACO (three planes), United African Airlines (three planes), Cargosour (two planes), Heavylift Cargo Airlines (two aircraft), Westinghouse Electric Corporation (two aircraft), Katale Aero Transport (one aircraft), Redcoat Air Cargo (one aircraft) and Royal Air Maroc (one aircraft).[12]

The Bristol 175 Britannia 312F with registration LV-JNL, seen after a crash-landing at Ezeiza, on 12 July 1970. (Edgardo Luzzi via Esteban Raczynski)

Another view of the same aircraft, seen during the process of 'cannibalisation': removal of all useful parts. The radome with the weather radar had already been removed. (Alex Reinhard via Gabriel Pavlovcic and Michael Magnusson)

The gross weight transported by TAR grew steadily, going from 22,346 tons in 1977 to 23,467 tons in 1978 and 30,315 tons in 1979. It is not surprising, therefore, that by 1979 the company was considered one of the most important in the world, being that strangely, it had its operational base in the southern confinement of the planet.[13]

The maximum expansion of the combined TAR and AER fleet was suddenly hampered by a lack of spare parts, a problem that was already becoming chronic for all Canadair CL-44 users around the world. The most critical parts on the Swingtail were the windshield, landing gear tyres and main gear lock hydraulic actuator. To get out of the bind, TAR and other operators formed a pool to commission the firm Bendix Aviation to manufacture some 50 tyres, while Martínez Guerrero asked his friend Hugo Hurtado, an excellent Argentine mechanic living in Miami, to manufacture the virtually unbreakable lock actuators. Solving the windshield problem was more delicate, since each replacement unit was made to order and cost more than $10,000 so the planes had to fly for more than a year with chipped cabin windows waiting for replacements.

Strictly speaking, Carlos Martínez Guerrero had recognised the problem of spare parts since 1970 as the low number of Swingtails produced made it clear that at some point, their replacement components were going to start to run out. However, the intensive use of these freighters by the world fleet, made this time shorten, so by 1977, the shortage was distressing. When TAR exhausted its stock of critical components, it reached into AER's warehouses and then entered into successive Aircraft Engine Short-Term Lease Agreements, Swap Agreements and even a pool of spare parts and engines with other companies using the model (Pooling Agreement). George Batchelor was involved in all these deals, simply because his company had purchased all the stock of spare parts for the demobilised CC-106 Yukon of the Canadian Armed Forces from the Crown Assets Disposal Corporation of Canada along with all the stock of spare parts for the model from Canadair Limited CL-44 once its production line was discontinued in 1965. Before the lack of spare parts reached a terminal point, Martínez Guerrero proposed to Tola to gradually convert the fleet of CL-44 and CC-106 turboprop aircraft to jets. TAR (and also from AER).

The proposal was not shared by Tola, nor by other shareholders, who considered that the companies were not yet prepared to support jet freighters such as the Douglas DC-8 or Boeing 707. It was not just about buying the planes, it was necessary to change the operating environment of turboprops, reorganise personnel selection and training processes, incorporate new tooling into the maintenance workshop and adopt the dynamics of recurrent training in flight simulators. As an alternative to the jets, Tola proposed to acquire turboprop freighters of greater capacity than the Yukon or Swingtail. As a result, serious progress was made in negotiations to buy two Douglas C-133 Cargomasters that had been deprogrammed from the Military Air Transport Service of the USAF after the incorporation

Canadair CL-44 Yukon with registration LV-JSY, which was lost in an accident at Miami International, on 27 May 1975. (via Roberto Gainnedu)

After being registered as LV-JZR, the Canadair CL-44-6 (ex-CC-106 Yukon with number 106926) flew very little with the Aerotransportes Entre Ríos. Shown here in February 1974 at Miami International. In March 1975, it was sold to Aeronaves del Peru, which registered it as OD-R-1005 on 26 June 1975. (Mercelo W. Miranda)

A Canadair CL-44 Yukon registration LV-JZB, seen in colours of Transporte Aéreo Rioplatense. This aircraft was lost in an accident at Carrasco Airport, outside Montevideo on 10 October 1979. (Werner Fischdick)

of the Lockheed C-5 Galaxy. The Cargomaster was a huge plane, with an extraordinarily large hold that could carry up to 50 tons of cargo over 4,000 miles. Tola had the opportunity to inspect two copies at the Davis-Monthan Air Force Base in Tucson, Arizona and returned, delighted with them. However, the negotiations did not advance due to the political differences that arose between the governments of Argentina and the United States after the coup de state of 24 March 1976.

Nevertheless, the frustration of the purchase ended up being beneficial as the C-133 had a structure with limited life (10,000 hours of use later extended to 19,000) and a poor design that caused fatigue due to severe vibrations and a tendency to spin at low speeds. On the other hand, the low number of Cargomasters built (barely 50 aircraft) made the imminent lack of spare parts foreseeable, a serious problem that by then, was well known to TAR and AER, since they suffered it daily with their Cl-44-6 freighters. and CL-44D.[14] [15]

Therefore, the position of Carlos Martínez Guerrero triumphed and the option to replace the fleet was consolidated in jet freighters. Thus, in mid-1977, TAR requested authorisation from the National Directorate of Commercial Air Transport, to incorporate a Boeing 707 freighter. The authorisation was granted by Resolution No. 31/78 of 4 January 1978 and six months later, on 7 July 1978, the company registered in its name, with the registration LV-MSG, the Boeing 707-321C serial 18591 /341. The plane was named Gloria in honour of the wife of Carlos Martínez Guerrero, who flew it to Ezeiza from the United States after having taken the simulator courses that allowed her to operate it.[16]

3

AN ARGENTINE AIRCRAFT TO DEVIL´S CAULDRON

In mid-1977, TAR requested authorisation from the National Directorate of Commercial Air Transport to incorporate a Boeing 707 freighter. The authorisation was granted by Resolution No. 31/78 of 4 January 1978 and six months later, on 7 July 1978, the company registered in its name, with the registration LV-MSG, the Boeing 707-321C serial 18591 /341. The plane was named Gloria in honour of the wife of Carlos Martínez Guerrero, who flew it to Ezeiza from the United States after having taken the simulator courses that allowed her to operate it.

The success of the jet was such that, barely five months after incorporating the Gloria, TAR was already determined to add a second Boeing 707, for which reason it submitted the request for a fleet expansion to the Dirección Nacional de Transporte Aéreo Comercial (DNTAC), the Argentine Air Force dependence in charge of Commercial Air Transport. The authorisation came on 14 February 1979 through Resolution No. 107/79, so negotiations for the purchase began immediately. On 30 November 1979, TAR registered its second jet in the National Aircraft Registry, which turned out to be the Boeing 707-338C serial number 19297/636, which began to bear the Argentine civil registration LV-MZE. The plane, named San Jorge, would arrive at Ezeiza on 29 December 1979, just in time to celebrate the tenth anniversary of the company's foundation.[1]

With two jet planes in service, TAR could afford to continue operating for a few more years, the two remaining Canadair four-engines (the LV-JTN and the LV-JZM), since it had spare parts from the LV-LBS of Aerotransportes Entre Ríos, which had been cannibalised in Ezeiza since 1978. It was clear that the time of the great

Carlos Martínez Guerrero, founder of the TAR, in the cockpit of the CL-44 registration LV-JTN. (Héctor Biondini)

Loading process of heavy merchandise into a Canadair CL-44 Swingtail of TAR, with registration LV-JZM. (FitzGerald Family)

Boeing 707-321C with registration LV-MSG, as seen in full colours of TAR, at the Basle/Mulhouse International, in France on 10 July 1978. (Eduard Marmet)

An advertisement published by Transporte Aéreos Rioplatense in all the main Argentine newspapers in July 1978, on the occasion of incorporation of its first freighter jet, the Boeing 707 with registration LV-MSG, named 'Gloria' (in homage to the wife of Carlos Martínez Guerrero). (Pablo Potenze)

Canadian dinosaurs was coming to an end and it was convenient to finish integrating the fleet combined with jets before the meteorite of extinction fell. Thus, AER also requested authorisation from the DNTAC to buy its own jet plane, a Boeing 707-321C freighter identical to the Gloria. However, the plane was not finally acquired because AER could not show the necessary economic solvency, nor could TAR support it, since she was concentrating on paying for her second jet.[2]

The incorporation of the two Boeing 707s produced the effect that Martínez Guerrero had foreseen, since it not only guaranteed the survival of TAR in the face of the limitations of spare parts for the CL-44, but also gave the company the possibility of carrying the same volume of cargo as a Swingtail at almost double the speed, which resulted in a greater number of contracts and increasingly satisfied customers. Thus, starting in July 1978, the company began to rationalise the use of its two remaining Canadian turboprops, using them only for the transfer of loads that justified the use of the folding tail, or to fulfil contracts that circumstantially, could not be served by the jets.

In July 1979, TAR was hired by the Argentine company Akapol S.A. to carry out five, long-distance flights between Buenos Aires and Tehran, each one with 35 tons of epoxy resins and Poxipol glue. It was not the first time that TAR had flown to Iran, as it had done so four years earlier from Rotterdam, in the Netherlands, at the request of the English company Transmeridian, which had run out of planes to complete the last of 10 flights transporting fresh eggs to Tehran. Since TAR had a CL-44 parked in Turin awaiting delayed cargo, it immediately responded to the request of its British ally, arriving on time at Mehrabad International Airport with the last shipment of 28 tons. With that background under his belt, Carlos Martínez Guerrero accepted the Akapol contract without hesitation, which affected the two Boeing 707s of his company.[3]

Advertisement for Transport Aéreo Rioplatense reporting the installation of noise-suppression kits on one of its Boeing 707 freighters (probably the LV-MZE), which allowed it to fly all around the world, including the USA, without restrictions. (Pablo Potenze)

The five flights to Tehran departed from Ezeiza on 16 July, 12 September, 16 October, 15 November 1979 and 6 February 1980, in all cases with prior overflight authorisation from the countries between Argentina and Iran. It was a normal request for freighters, whose management was in the hands of the National Directorate of Air Transport and the Ministry of Foreign Affairs of the Nation.[4]

The flights taking epoxy resin to Tehran were the farthest made so far by TAR (or by any other Argentine cargo). In addition to this, they occurred in truly turbulent times for the destination country, which by then was submerged in the political and economic disorder resulting from the so-called Islamic Revolution that had consolidated its power on 11 February 1979. This gave rise to the Islamic Republic of Iran, a fundamentalist theocracy that, through the overthrow of Shah Mohamed Reza Pahlavi, put an end to a 25-century-old Persian empire. It was in that context and with operating experience on long-haul flights to the Far East, that these combined would open the door to one of the most controversial episodes in the company's history.

It was the emergence of the Islamic Republic of Iran, which from the outset declared itself an ardent enemy of the United States, that generated an immediate economic embargo decreed by the government of Washington. The measure involved the freezing of Iranian assets in US banks, the limitation of exports of US products to Iran and the reduction in the purchase of Persian oil, which was the country's main exportable resource.

However, where the impact of the US embargo was most noticeable was in the interruption of the supply of spare parts to the enormous arsenal accumulated by the Shah, the vast majority purchased from US suppliers. During the reign of the deposed monarch, the Imperial Iranian Air Force received a total of 440 combat aircraft, 90 transports and 170 helicopters. For his army, the Shah ordered more than 600 Chieftain tanks and 200 Scorpion tanks from Great Britain, to which were added another 750 M-47, M-48 and M-60 tanks of American origin, plus some 500 helicopters for combat tasks, links, transport and anti-tank attack.

The Iranian combat aircraft whose spare parts were hit by the US embargo, included 260 McDonnell-Douglas R/F-4D/E Phantom II fighter-bombers, 75 Grumman F-14A Tomcat fighter-interceptors, 55 Northrop F-5E/ F Tigers, two Lockheed P-3F Orion ocean exploration aircraft, one Boeing 747 command and control aircraft, 20 Boeing/Meridionali CH-47C Chinook heavy helicopters, 10 Kaman HH-43 Huskie helicopters, two Agusta-Sikorsky S assault helicopters -61, an Agusta-Sikorsky SH-3D Sea King transport helicopter and two Sikorsky RH-53D troop transport helicopters. This formidable combat aircraft was completed with 13 Boeing 707-300 tanker planes, dozens of Lockheed C-130 Hercules cargo planes, Bell 205 Huey, Bell 206 JetRanger, Bell 212, Bell 214 troop transport helicopters and attack helicopters and a Bell AH-1J Huey Cobra.[5]

For Iran's neighbours, the Islamic Revolution was a total threat, not only because Islamic fundamentalism was irreducible but because it threatened to undermine political power in their own countries. Specifically, this was the fear of the president of Iraq, Saddam Hussein, for whom the only alternative to prevent this disaster was to resort to a military option and to stop the Islamic Revolution with weapons. This meant invading Iran, overthrowing the revolutionary government of Ayatollah Khomeini and restoring the reign of the Pahlavi dynasty, since for Iraq it was preferable to face a pro-Western dynastic monarch than a revolutionary

Iraqi president Saddam Hussein during a press conference in Baghdad, on 11 November 1980. (AP)

fundamentalist cleric. Saddam was confident that in the process, he would receive the support of the United States and its Western allies, shifting to Baghdad the meridian of regional geopolitical power, which during the Shah's reign, had passed through Tehran. The Iraqi invasion of Iran would allow, incidentally, to settle forever an historic border dispute between Iran and Iraq: sovereignty over the Arvandrud/Shatt al-Arab river. This received the waters of the Tigris and Euphrates rivers to dump them into the Gulf Persian, whose margins would be definitively incorporated into Iraqi territory, as well as the adjacent Iranian province of Khuzestan, extremely rich in oil reserves.[6]

Iraqi intelligence calculated that Persian resistance to an invasion would be weak or non-existent as the Islamic Revolution government had produced a gigantic purge of the top brass of its armed forces. It had viewed them as addicted to the deposed Shah, even going so far as to execution of hundreds of officers from the Army, Navy and Imperial Air Force, already numb for lack of spare parts.

The Iraqi invasion of Iran began on 22 September 1980, with surprise air raids on Tehran's Mehrabad airport and 10 other Iranian airfields, which sought to destroy the Persian Air Force on the ground. Thus began the Iran-Iraq War, a fierce conflict that was to last for almost eight years, until 20 August 1988. The invasion enjoyed the tacit or express support of the United States, Great Britain and France, which did not condemn in any way, the act of aggression. However, things did not turn out as Saddam Hussein expected; the Arabs who inhabited the Iranian province of Khuzestan, did not rise up against Ayatollah Khomeini nor did they legitimise the Iraqi invasion. In addition, the Persian resistance was fierce, particularly in the city of Khorramshahr, where 7,000 deaths were recorded on each side. What surprised the invaders most was the reaction of the Iranian Air Force, which retaliated just the next day with a full-scale attack on Arab airbases and infrastructure. Groups of Mc Donnell-Douglas F-4 Phantom II and Northrop Grumman F-5 Tiger jets attacked targets throughout Iraq, including oil installations, dams, chemical plants and refineries. Retaliatory airstrikes included the Iraqi airbases in Mosul and Baghdad and the Kirkuk refinery.[7, 8]

Time gained by the Iranian Air Force allowed the Persian Army to reorganise, and in January 1981, Iranian ground forces began a counter-attack. The push stalled after three days, mainly due to a lack of spare parts to keep moving the columns of tanks and trucks pressing the invaders. The stalemate lasted for the next nine months, except for intense artillery duels and sporadic ground offensives by both sides, which failed to move the front line. The shortage of spare parts, which had reached a critical level on the ground, also began to be felt in the Iranian Air Force. The Bell AH-1 Cobra helicopters, which had done so much damage to the invading tanks, were barely

This photograph taken on 16 July 1979, shows the Boeing 707 with registration LV-MSG, spooling up its engines at the Ezeiza International, at the start of the first of its five cargo flights to Iran. (Héctor Biondini)

operational anymore. The powerful F-4 Phantom II fighter-bombers, on whose backs the Iranian offensive effort fell, were severely conditioned and had also begun the process of cannibalisation. The powerful Grumman F-14 Tomcat fighters, then the most modern interceptors in the world, were unable to unfold their full potential due to a lack of spare parts for their radars, navigation systems and the microprocessors of their lethal Phoenix missiles. In this context, the Iranian government authorised its intelligence services to explore any alternative or supply channel that would allow its armed forces to access the spare parts they badly needed to continue in the war. This included buying them clandestinely on the international black market.[9]

4

FOR THE SAME PRICE, OSIRAK

In the aftermath of the 1979 Islamic Revolution, the fledgling Islamic Republic of Iran took the most radical anti-Jewish position imaginable in the Muslim world, calling directly for the elimination of the State of Israel.[1] [2] However, relations between Iran and Israel had been very good until the Revolution. From the establishment of the State of Israel in 1948 until 1979, Israel and Iran maintained close diplomatic relations. Iran was, after Turkey, the second sovereign state with a Muslim majority to recognise the nascent state of Israel. From then on, Israel saw Iran as its natural ally, a non-Arab power on the very edge of the Arab world with which to engage strongly following David Ben Gurion's geopolitical vision. [3]

For his part, the Shah of Iran, Mohammad Reza Pahlavi, saw Israel as a counterbalance against its historical Arab rivals and therefore favoured the multiplication of trade agreements with Israel. This shared geopolitical vision enabled the joint development of major undertakings such as the construction in 1968 of the Trans-Israel pipeline, other port facilities by the Israeli Eilat Ahskelon Pipeline Company (EAPC) and the National Iranian Oil Company (NIOC).

In the late 1970s, the Imperial Iranian Air Force and its Jewish counterpart, the Heyl Ha'Avir, had in their inventory a large number of common, American-made aircraft. The Jews had purchased from the United States 204 McDonnell-Douglas F-4E Phantom II fighter-bombers plus 12 RF-4E photo-reconnaissance examples, 48 Bell AH-1G/S/Q Cobra attack helicopters, 30 Hughes 500MD helicopters, 24 Lockheed C-130E/H Hercules cargo planes, two KC-130H tankers, 10 Boeing 707s, 34 Bell 205 tactical helicopters, 20 Bell 206 reconnaissance helicopters, 12 Bell 212 combat helicopters, and 24 Sikorsky S-heavy helicopters 65C/CH-53D.

The models of the Israeli and Iranian air forces were completely compatible with each other, in the same way that the tactics and strategies for the use of the material were compatible, as the pilots of both countries had received training by the same instructors at the same bases. Even better, the intelligence services of both armed forces were closely linked, which ultimately played in favour of Iran when its territory was invaded on 22 September 1980 by the bellicose Iraqi president Saddam Hussein. [4]

It is not surprising, therefore, that at the beginning of 1981, when the Islamic Republic of Iran went looking for spare parts on the black market that would allow it to keep its tanks, planes, and helicopters in service in the midst of the war it was waging with Iraq, Persian intelligence services would point directly to Israel as a primary source of supply. However, it was not possible to negotiate directly with Israel, not only because the government that emerged from the Islamic Revolution had severed all diplomatic and political ties with Tel Aviv, but also because the Iranian revolutionary government itself did not recognise the legitimacy of Israel as a state. Buying arms from Israel meant not only accepting the entity of the State of Israel, but also giving up ideologically, to a rival whom Ayatollah Khomeini considered an even worse enemy than the Iraqis with whom he was at war.

Nevertheless, the need for supplies increased with each passing day and Iranian intelligence services, in contact with their Israeli counterparts, confirmed that a secret deal was possible. In this context, Ayatollah Khomeini authorised the talks to be conducted by Dr. Sadeq Tabatabai, one of his most trusted advisers on sensitive issues.

Tabatabai was one of the most influential people in the Islamic Revolution. Graduating as a biochemist in West Germany, at the age of 32 he obtained a doctorate at the Universität Aachen in the fields of enzymology and genetics, going on to work as a professor at Bochum Universität. He was one of the strongest intellectuals that the critical movement against the Shah had and his predicament reached the highest strata of the European intellectual and academic community. During Ayatollah Khomeini's years of exile, Dr. Tabatabai was co-editor of the Muslim Student magazine, which was published in West Germany between 1974 and 1979, as well as a founder and member of the Association of Islamic Student Communities in Europe, the United States and Canada.

These political activities and his intelligence earned Dr. Tabatabai the confidence of the Ayatollah, which was further consolidated when his sister, Fatima Tabatabai, married Sayyud Ahmad Khomeini, son

Ayatollah Ruhollah Khomeini, seen being helped to descend from a Boeing 747 of Iran Air at Tehran's Mehrabad International, on 1 February 1978, after 14 years in exile. Visible on the far right of the photograph is Dr. Sadeq Tabatabai, the right-hand man of the Iranian leader, who was to play a key role in the secret negotiations with Israel of 1980 – a state considered 'Little Satan' by Khomeini. (UPI)

Carlos Martínez Guerrero in the captain's seat of the Boeing 707 with registration LV-MSG, shown during one of the stopovers between Buenos Aires and Tehran. (Oscar Bellini)

The Boeing 707 with registration LV-MSG ('Gloria') of TAR, seen on the commercial platform of Tehran's Mehrabad International, in July 1979. The jet was in the process of delivering a shipment dispatched by the company Akapol S. A. (Oscar Bellini)

of Ruhollah Khomeini himself. It is not surprising, therefore, that Tabatabai was part of the inner circle that accompanied Khomeini on his famous return flight to Iran on 12 February 1979. Since then, he held various political positions in the government of the nascent Islamic Republic of Iran, standing out in all due to its proximity to the supreme leader of the Revolution. Appointing him to lead the secret talks on the arms issue meant, quite simply, that to talk to him was to talk to Khomeini himself. [5, 6]

Dr. Sadeq Tabatabai introduced himself to the Jews as 'a representative of the Iranian Revolution Defence Council,' the central body of Iran's most important intelligence and security system. On the Israeli side, the first liaison who paved the way for negotiation was Ari Ben-Menashe, an Iranian Jew born in Tehran in 1951, whose parents were both Iraqi Jews. Ben-Menashe had immigrated to Israel in his teens, joining the Signals Intelligence division of the Israel Defence Forces in 1974. Fluent in Persian, Arabic, Hebrew and English, he became a key player in the Israeli Military Intelligence Directorate, serving on it for 10 years from 1977.

Backing Ben-Menashe was the Israeli military and political hierarchy, including Prime Minister Menachem Beghin, Israel Defence Forces Chief-of-Staff General Rafael Eitan, and General Yitzhak Hofi, Director of HaMosad leModi'in ulTafkidim Meyuhadim, the Israel Institute for Intelligence and Special Operations, better known by its acronym Mossad. It was immediately clear to everyone that the issue that had arisen with Iran was not only sensitive but terribly complex, which is why the so-called Joint Committee for Israel-Iran Relations was formed, with representatives from Mossad and each of the armed forces.[7]

For the Mossad, the Joint Committee was made up of the aforementioned General Yitzhak Hofi, General Nahum Admoni (deputy director of the Mossad) and General Zvi Zamir (director of the Mossad between 1968 and 1974 and since then, his liaison with the Defence Forces From Israel). These were men with souls of steel and blood of ice, all veterans of war with records of service as stunning as they were flawless. General Hofi had commanded a company in the 1948 Arab-Israeli War and had led the IDF Northern Command during the 1973 Yom Kippur War. General Admoni had fought in the 1948 war and had been fighting ever since. served as an intelligence officer, executing, supervising, or planning a large number of secret Mossad operations. General Zamir had also fought in the 1948 war as an infantry platoon leader, had become a reconnaissance pilot and years later, had risen to the position of head of the Southern Command of the Israel Defence Forces. Each one separately was a true talent, but together they formed an unbeatable team.

Following secret instructions from the Joint Committee, in early February 1981 agent Ari Ben-Menashe flew to Vienna, Austria, to talk unofficially with his old childhood friend Sayeed Mehdi Kashani about the possibility of supplying Jewish weapons to the Islamic regime in Tehran. The proposal was concrete and consisted of the offer of spare parts and avionics for F-4 Phantom II aircraft, 300,000 122-mm artillery ammunition, 51-mm mortars and rockets for the infantry, 100,000 Kalashnikov AK-47 machine guns with ammunition and air-to-surface missiles. The Iranians needed engines for their British Chieftain tanks and Israel had 1,000 German-made units in stock ready for mounting in its own tanks. Each engine had been purchased for between 30 thousand and 40 thousand dollars. Israel offered them to Iran at the exorbitant price of $450,000 each. The final total of the operation amounted to one billion dollars, with a net benefit for Israel of 50 percent on the total cost of the goods sold. The Iranians agreed to analyse the proposal and days later, let the Jews know that the answer would be given personally in Iran. [8]

Thus, in mid-February 1981, Ari Ben-Menashe, with a false passport in the name of Canadian businessman William Grace, arrived in Tehran via Vienna on an Iran Air flight. He was discreetly transferred from the Mehrabad International Airport to the Islamic Consultative Assembly building (the Iranian Parliament or Majlis).

Generals Nahum Admoni (left), Zvi Zamir (centre) and Yitzhak Hofi (right), heads of Israeli intelligence in 1981. They were in charge of the delicate planning of the secret supply of US weapons from Israel to Iran, which received the name Operation Seashell. (Guido Ghiretti)

Unloading boxes of Poxipol glue and drums of epoxy resins shipped by Akapol S. A. to Tehran, in February 1980. The TAR used its two Boeing 707s for all such flights. (Oscar Bellini)

In a small room he met with Ayatollah Akbar Hashemí Rafsanjani, the most influential member of the Council of the Islamic Revolution after Ayatollah Khomeini himself, possessing a cunning superior to that of the rest of the actors in the political scene of post-revolutionary Iran. Joining Ayatollah Hashemí was Colonel Javad Fakouri, commander of the Iranian Air Force since June 1980.

After an icy presentation, the men went straight to the point: Iran accepted without haggling, the price imposed for the spare parts and weapons that Israel promised to supply, but the cost of freight and transport insurance should be included in the amount, with the corresponding coverage for war risk. Ben-Menashe did not see that the matter could constitute a problem but agreed to immediately communicate the counter-proposal to his superiors. As the conversation progressed, it came to the matter of logistics. At that time, Ben-Menashe proposed the masquerade of chartering a plane from 'an Argentine company that could fly to Tel Aviv,' although he did not specify the identity of the company.

What did become clear was that the commissioned pilots had to submit a flight plan at the 'Ben Gurion' International Airport bound for Portugal and over Cyprus, change their route to Tehran. The secrecy surrounding each flight was to be such that not even Israeli air traffic controllers should know what the final destination of the cargo planes would be. The Iranians agreed, leaving the planning and execution details to their suppliers. When all the points on the agenda had been exhausted, Ben-Menashe said goodbye with the same poker face with which he had arrived. Back in Tel Aviv, he reported in great detail what had been discussed with the Persians. It became clear to the Jews that Iran was on the brink of disintegration. With Ben-Menashe's information on the table, the Joint Committee accepted the Iranian counter-proposal and gave the green light to the secret supply of weapons to Iran under the code name Operation Seashell.

In the midst of the secret talks held in Tehran, the Iranians slipped in a proposal that immediately caught Israeli attention. It included the possibility of the provision of Israeli intelligence information about Osirak – the Iraqi nuclear reactor against which the Persians had launched an unsuccessful air attack – in the price of the arms purchase.

The Iraqi nuclear programme dated back to 1956, when the US-supported Atoms for Peace project was launched to establish nuclear research programmes in various allied nations. A few years later, in 1962, the Iraqis launched their own independent nuclear programme by building their first reactor, a two-megawatt IRT-5000 supplied by the Soviet Union. This reactor, built in Tuwaitha, 19km southeast of Baghdad, went critical in 1967 and was upgraded to five megawatts in 1978.

The agreement for the construction of two new reactors, to be built together with the existing IRT-5000, was signed by Saddam Hussein and the President of France, Jacques Chirac, in September 1975. In France, the project was called Osiris, but it became to be known as Osirak, with an obvious reference to the receiving country. In Iraq, the two reactors became known as Tammuz-1 and Tammuz 2. Tammuz-1 was a light water reactor for materials research and testing, with a power output rated at 40 megawatts but capable of reaching 70 megawatts, making it one of the largest of its kind in the world. Tammuz-2 (Isis to the French) was a low power reactor for research and training purposes. The construction of the infrastructure was completed between 1976 and 1979 and thereafter, the Iraqis and French began to build the main body of the first reactor itself.

In Israel, the debate on the strategy to adopt in response to the development of the Iraqi reactor, began to take place during the first term of Prime Minister Yitzhak Rabin (1974 –1977), a period

Israeli Prime Minister Menachem Begin (left) in talks with his Defence Minister Ariel Sharon. Under the leadership of both, the secret arms supply agreements for their arch-enemy Iran were organised. Between 2001 and 2006, Sharon served as the Prime Minister of Israel. (Israeli Government Press Office)

during which planning and training began to conduct an air raid to destroy it. [9] Preparations intensified after the change of government and the inauguration in 1977 of the new Prime Minister Menachim Begin, who authorised the construction of a full-scale Iraqi reactor building so that Jewish pilots could practice their bombing. During these training missions, three Israeli pilots died in accidents. The operation was fairly polished when, in October 1980, the Mossad informed Begin that the Osirak reactor could be operational by June 1981. This assessment was significantly supported by reconnaissance photographs from the US Lockheed KH-2 spy satellites. 11 Kennan launched into space on 14 June 1978 and 7 February 1980. On 30 November 1980, just eight days after the Iraqi invasion began, the Iranian Air Force carried out an attack on the Al-Tuwaitha facility with two F-4 Phantom IIs, which caused various damage although they failed to stop the development of the Tammuz 1 and 2 reactors. [10,, 11,, 12,, 13]

With this negative background, the issue of the destruction of the Osirak reactor was put back on the table at the end of February 1981 during the secret negotiations for the sale of Israeli arms to the Islamic government of Tehran. Colonel Javad Fakouri, Commander-in-Chief of the Iranian Air Force, proposed that as part of the package to be negotiated, Israel would commit to destroy Iraqi nuclear facilities. For this purpose, it was in a position to supply all the intelligence information collected before and after the failed air raid on 30 November 1980. The Israelis discussed the proposal and responded that the operation was possible, but that their jets might need landing permits in Iran if they were intercepted by Iraqi aircraft or if they ran out of fuel in the return flight to Israeli territory. The mere idea of a Jewish warplane refuelling at a Persian airfield was enough to make the skin twitch of any Iranian fundamentalist and particularly the clerics promoting the Islamic Revolution; the negotiations had to go to another level.

The issue was extremely sensitive as Iraq was at war with Iran, not with Israel, so a Jewish attack could trigger a regional escalation of the conflict. However, Saddam Hussein had repeatedly declared his enmity towards Israel, so it was not unreasonable to think that he would use a nuclear weapon on Jewish cities as viciously or more viciously than on Iranian cities. The possibility of attacking the Iraqi nuclear power plant was escalating in hierarchy until it reached the knowledge of the Israeli Prime Minister, Menachem Begin, who personally authorised a pre-emptive attack under the name of Operation Opera. The details of the mission were so sensitive and secret that they could not even be known by middle managers. For this reason, in mid-March 1981 Sayeed Mehdi Kashani and Colonel Javad Fakouri arranged a meeting between the President of Iran, Abolhassan Bani-Sadr and Professor Moshe Arens, Israel's ambassador to the United States and a man with whom Begin had extreme confidence.

The six-hour meeting took place in a hotel in Nice, France. Arens flew direct from New York to Nice on a commercial Pan Am flight while Bani-Sadr flew on a private jet from Tehran via Paris. In the course of the conclave, the date of the attack on the Iraqi reactor was set for 7 June 1981. There was additional Iranian intelligence support for the operation and permission for Jewish planes to land at an Iranian airfield located in Tabrizin case of emergency. The Iranian Air Force immediately provided the Jewish aerial photographs taken of the Al-Tuwaitha compound on 30 November 1980 by an McDonnell-Douglas RF-4E Phantom II stationed at Nojeh Air Base. It became clear that after the attack, Iran would condemn the violation of its airspace by Israel, which would remain solely responsible for the episode.

Iranian President Abolhassan Bani-Sadr (third from the left, centre with glasses and moustache) inspecting an AH-1 Cobra attack helicopter of the Iranian Army Aviation, in February 1981. By then, it was clear that Iran could not continue to resist without solving the pressing problem of spare parts. (AP)

Both the supply of weapons and the air attack on the nuclear power plant were on condition of payment by Iran of the agreed price; the transfers were made immediately. The Iranian black money was deposited in five different numbered accounts, each worth 200 million dollars, at the Girozentrale Vienna bank, one of Austria's leading financial companies, which was chosen for its ease of transferring assets to branches in Britain, Switzerland, Italy, Spain, United States, Hong Kong, Australia and Eastern Europe countries. As soon as the Persians deposited their promise, the Israeli Air Force carried out a reconnaissance mission of the Osirak reactor, a result of which, excellent aerial photos of all the buildings of the Iraqi atomic complex were obtained. The copies for the Iranians were forwarded through the military attaché at the Israeli embassy in Paris, who forwarded them to Persian intelligence through contact agent Simon Gabbay. This formally closed the commitment made regarding the provision of intelligence information but immediately opened a new circle within the Israeli government, which began to wonder what would happen if Israel itself – and not Iran – attacked and destroyed the Osirak nuclear power plant.

With the updated photographs of the Al-Tuwaitha complex, the Israelis finished planning their attack on the Osirak reactor, giving precise shape to the so-called Operation Opera. The distance between the Israeli airfields and the target was more than 1,600km and to cover it, the attacking planes had to necessarily violate the airspace of Jordan and Saudi Arabia. Although the attack practices carried out since 1979 had been carried out with McDonnell-Douglas A-4M Skyhawk fighter-bombers, the final mission was assigned to eight General Dynamics F-16A/B Fighting Falcons. These were part of a batch of 160 units that, paradoxically, had been acquired by the Shah of Iran, then caught up in the US military embargo following the Islamic Revolution and immediately handed over by the United States to the Israeli Air Force, which began receiving them on 31 January 1981. The attack formation would be protected by several McDonnell-Douglas F-15 Eagles that would provide air cover. [14, 15]

Operation Opera began at Etzion Air Base at 15:55 on 7 June 1981. To avoid detection, the Israeli pilots spoke Arabic with a Saudi accent while flying over Jordanian airspace, telling air traffic controllers they were part of a Saudi patrol that had lost its way. Instead, while flying within Saudi Arabian airspace, they posed as Jordanian pilots, using radio signals and formations similar to those employed by the Jordanian Air Force. Once depleted, the supplemental fuel tanks were ejected during the outbound flight over the desert of the Arabian peninsula.[16]

At 18:35 local time and 20km from the Al-Tuwaitha complex, the F-16 formation climbed to an altitude of 2,100 metres and then descended towards the reactor at a speed of 1,100km/h. A little over a kilometre from the target, the planes began to drop their bombs, two at five-second intervals. At least eight of the 16 hit the reactor's enclosing dome. Once the mission was accomplished, the squadron was climbing until it reached its economic cruising level and began its return to Israel. [17, 18]

The attack against the Al-Tuwaitha compound, which lasted less than two minutes, forever liquidated Saddam Hussein's nuclear aspirations and incidentally, allowed Menachem Begin's party, the Likud, to retain power after winning the parliamentary elections of 30 June 1981. Above all, Operation Opera generated in the highest echelons of the Jewish and Persian governments, the feeling of mutual trust that they so badly needed in order to carry out the secret traffic in arms and spare parts between Israel and Iran. This was a matter so delicate that, if it became known, it could cost the heads of Iranian President Abolhassan Bani-Sadr and Colonel Javad Fakouri. During the times of the Islamic Revolution, it was not even conceivable that the Iranian Air Force or Army was buying the 'Little Satan' weapons manufactured by the 'Great Satan'.

5
THE STRANGE WORLD OF JACK

In order that the movements of Operation Seashell could be shown to the public as a mere business of private actors, the Israeli intelligence service summoned the Swiss arms dealer Andreas Jenni, the English dealer Ian Smalley and the Portuguese dealer Angelo Caldas, who organised a kind of money table to finance the first clandestine flights. One of the investors was the Iranian Ahmed Heidari who disbursed 200,000 dollars to support a series of five or six flights that, it was already known, would be in charge of an Argentine transport company. Other investors included the Iranian Jew Youssof Azar and Dr. Sadeq Tabatabai, who participated through the shell company International Trading Centre, based in Frankfurt (then the Federal Republic of Germany).[1]

The cast of intermediaries and agents included Israelis (Ari Ben-Menashe, Ahran Moshell, Yaacov Nimrodi and Will Northrop), Americans (Richard Babayan, Richard Brenneke, William Herrmann, Oswald LeWinter, Heinrich Rupp and Gunther Russbacher), French (Robert Benes and Nicholas Ignatiew), Iranians (Jamshid Hashemí, Houshang Lavi, Hamid Naqashan), a Swiss (Hans Albert Kunz), a Portuguese (Carlos Vieira De Mello) and a South African (Dirk Stoffberg). All of them were dark characters, financiers and dealers born and raised in the shadows of the dark world of arms trafficking. They were also rich men and very well connected politically, since it was impossible to prosper in the arms business without solid contacts within the armed forces and the circles of power of the countries in need of supplies.[2]

This veritable constellation of shadowy characters occupied offices in Bonn, Paris, Amsterdam, London, Monte Carlo, Strasbourg and Tel Aviv. From there they projected a network of vital contacts into much more remote places like Ankara, Seoul, Taipei, Montevideo, Buenos Aires, São Paulo, Tripoli, Washington, San Diego, and Orlando. Only the Israeli intelligence service had full knowledge and control of the network, the links and the flow of funds, so that if one link was revealed. it was exceedingly difficult for the movement of the entire chain to be put at risk. The 'headquarters' of the agents and intermediaries was the bar of the Hotel President in Geneva, overlooking Lake Geneva, where they exchanged information, contracts and lists with requirements under

Dr. Saddeq Tabatabai speaking with Ayatollah Khomeini. Given his closeness and relationship of trust with the Shi'a leader, Tabatabai was in charge of conducting the secret negotiations with Israel in pursuit of weapons and spare parts that Iran so badly needed for defence from the Iraqi aggression. (AFP)

John McIvar Malloch, pilot, businessman, smuggler and arms dealer. One of his companies, Afro Continental Airways, was used to cover-up the secret transfers between Iran and Israel with help of the Canadair CL-44 transport with registration LV-JTN of Transporte Aéreo Rioplatense. (Alan Brough)

the protection of the legal regime of Switzerland, whose multitude of banks allowed diluting all the transfers between anonymous accounts and financial agents.

For air transport itself, the Mossad relied on John McIvar (Jack) Malloch, a South African resident of Rhodesia and former Royal Air Force pilot during the Second World War, whose public and clandestine adventures are truly endless. Depending on which source is consulted, Malloch is described as a superlative aviator, an energetic and tireless entrepreneur, a mercenary without codes, a modern air pirate, a soldier of fortune, an expert smuggler, an unscrupulous opportunist, an arms dealer, a Rhodesian patriot or simply a man trapped by his time and circumstances. Most likely, he was all of these at the same time or at different stages of his life. The truth is that both he and his planes were involved in the war in Yemen (flying for the British and the French), in the war in Sudan (flying for the British), in the war of secession in the former Belgian Congo (flying for the Katangese and against the United Nations), in the civil wars of independent Congo (flying for the CIA), in the Congolese mercenary revolts (flying for mercenary leaders Bob Denard and Mike Hoare), in the Biafran War (flying for the French secret service SDECE), in the coups in the Comoro Islands (flying again for Bob Denard), in the various crises in Rhodesia (flying for the Rhodesian government on arms trafficking missions, breaking the international blockade and direct military support) and in the clandestine supply of Israeli weapons to Iran (organising the logistics so that the flights were not detected).

John McIvar Malloch was born in Durban, South Africa, in October 1920. In 1925, his entire family moved to Umtali (present-day Mutare) in what was then the territory of Southern Rhodesia (present-day Zimbabwe), where they lived until 1943, when they travelled to Greater Britain to enlist in the Royal Air Force and participate in the Second World War. From December 1943, he flew various combat missions against the Nazis, until in February 1945, three months before the end of the war in Europe, he was shot down, wounded behind enemy lines in occupied Italy, captured by the Germans and rescued by the partisans. After the war, he returned to his native land, in January 1948 he married Zoe Coventry in Salisbury (now Harare) and in March 1951 he participated in the first flight of Supermarine Spitfire Mk.22 fighters destined for the Southern Rhodesian Air Force.[3]

In 1960, Jack Malloch organised the Rhodesian Air Services (RAS) airline with the aim of linking by air the five main cities of the country (Salisbury, Bulawayo, Chiredzi, Fort Victoria and Triangle), for which he used a De Havilland Dove, two Douglas C-47 Skytrains and a Douglas DC-4. The company was born in times of intense instability in the Central African region. Indeed, on 30 June 1960, the Kingdom of Belgium granted independence to its colonial domains in the Congo, giving rise to the birth of the Democratic Republic of the Congo and on 11 July 1960, its first black ruler was elected, Prime Minister Patrice Lumumba. That same day, his greatest political rival, Moise Kapenda Tshombé, declared the secession of the Congolese province of Katanga with the aim of turning it into an independent state but the new republic was not recognised by any country, giving rise to a frightful civil war in the course of which both sides dedicated themselves to carrying out veritable ethnic massacres.

In this context, Malloch's relationship with Tshombé began, which became much stronger as of 21 February 1961, when the United Nations Security Council issued Resolution No. 161 ordering the formation of an international force for stopping the ongoing civil war. Flying for Tshombé, Malloch dedicated himself to systematically violating the international air blockade and moving all kinds of weapons to the Katangese rebels. In July 1962, during one of those clandestine flights, United Nations forces shot down one of the Rhodesian Air Service Douglas C-47s over Katanga.

This did not stop Malloch's clandestine flights, much less his friendship with Tshombé, who, after being defeated by the United Nations Peacekeepers on 15 January 1963, went into exile in Northern Rhodesia (present-day Zambia) and later to Spain, from where he returned to the Democratic Republic of the Congo to be anointed as Prime Minister in June 1964. In that period and in the absence of a better client, between 1963 and 1964, the Rhodesian Air Service planes carried out dozens of clandestine flights of arms supply in Yemen. However, with Tshombé back in power, the demands for flights to and from the Congo increased and Malloch again found himself involved in secret flights, this time supplying by air, the anti-guerrilla missions of the Irish mercenary Thomas Michael Hoare (aka Mad Mike). His unit of 300 paid soldiers, the so-called 5 Commando de la Armée Nationale Congolaise, annihilated between August and November 1964 the rebels and Congolese guerrillas who were supporters of the assassinated Patrice Lumumba, who still opposed the shadowy government of Tshombé by force of arms.

Everything seemed to indicate that Jack Malloch's illegal flights had ended after the Congo crisis, but this was not the case, precisely due to the expansion of the independence processes in Central Africa. On 6 July 1964, the United Kingdom of Great Britain and Northern Ireland granted independence to its protectorate of Nyasaland, which became the Republic of Malawi. Three months later, on 24 October 1964, the territory of Northern Rhodesia also gained its independence, giving rise to the birth of the Republic of Zambia. The white population of Southern Rhodesia assumed that Great Britain would adopt the same temperament with that colony, which was definitely the best administered of all since it had a self-management regime in force since 1923. However, the discussions with London escalated in intensity and finally, on 11 November

1965, Southern Rhodesia (now called simply Rhodesia) unilaterally declared its independence from Great Britain, considering itself a sovereign state.

The British government did not respond with force to Rhodesia's unilateral declaration of independence; it was the second separate colony on its own since 1776, after the United States of America. London mobilised all its diplomatic resources so that the new country would not be recognised by the United Nations and applied strong economic sanctions, including the end of the exchange relationship between the pound sterling and the Rhodesian currency, the seizure of assets and the prohibition importation of tobacco from that territory. The United Nations imposed economic sanctions in 1968 after it adopted Resolution 216, which condemned the declaration of independence 'as being made by a racist minority' of 270,000 white Europeans seeking to impose their political will on 6 million native Africans. In the midst of almost complete international isolation, Rhodesia continued to be run as an unrecognised state, assisted by only two countries: South Africa (where the racist Apartheid regime still held sway) and Portugal (which did not wish to grant independence to its colony).

To break the international blockade of Rhodesia, its new Prime Minister, Ian Smith, an old Royal Air Force pilot, required the services of his compatriot Jack Malloch, who had foresightedly formed a new airline, Air Trans Africa, whose name was not known and had no relation to the independent territory. Moreover, Air Trans Africa was not incorporated in Rhodesia but in the Gabonese Republic, in whose aircraft register three aircraft were registered: a Lockheed Super Constellation, a Douglas C-54 and a De Havilland DH.114 Heron. The constitution of the company in Gabon had a very simple explanation. All of his planes and many of those that Malloch would buy in the future, were owned by Gabonese President Omar Bongo Ondimba, who had bought them through shell companies incorporated in the Principality of Liechtenstein.[4]

Malloch became a millionaire flying the blockade-breaking flights to Rhodesia, partly because Ian Smith's government absorbed all of Air Trans Africa's liabilities and partly because the cargo movement itself was profitable. Soon the chrome and beef from the independent territory began to flow normally to the United States and Europe. The planes also returned loaded, especially with weapons, since a guerrilla conflict had already broken out in Rhodesia between the white government forces and two rival black nationalist groups, both communist and both backed by the Soviet Union's lavish export arsenal.

Malloch was in the midst of a undercover supply to Rhodesia when, on 29 May 1967, the southeastern provinces of Nigeria decided to secede from that country to form the Republic of Biafra. Nigeria resisted secession and on 6 July 1967, the so-called Biafran War began, which would last until 15 January 1970. It was a true humanitarian massacre in the course of which, the Nigerian forces gambled on weakening the Biafran population and generating an appalling famine that claimed hundreds of thousands of lives. Malloch used his planes to supply the Biafran rebels with food and weapons. In fact, the first arms supply flight to the newborn Republic of Biafra was carried out in July 1967 by one of his planes.

As was to be expected, the operations became increasingly reckless and dangerous, since it was not just a question of forging papers or circumventing administrative procedures (as in the blockade of Rhodesia) but of facing direct Nigerian fire. For this reason, Malloch's pilots specialised in night raids and low-altitude drops, for which purpose the Lockheed Super Constellation were particularly useful, whose side door could be opened inwards, facilitating the release of cargo mid-flight. All the Super Constellations that Malloch was acquiring to serve the airlift to Biafra, as well as the Douglas DC-7s bought for the same purpose, flew with their licence plates covered with paper and adhesive tape so that their origin could not be identified and in turn, for the Gabon government to continue financing the purchase of new aircraft.

Between July and November 1967, in parallel with the covert flights to Biafra, Jack Malloch's freighter fleet was again compromised in the Congo, this time to supply the forces of the Belgian mercenary Jean Schramme (alias Black Jack). During the mutiny, he led with his unit of soldiers of fortune, the 10 Commando de la Armée Nationale Congolaise. Matters escalated on 30 June 1967 when the private jet Hawker-Siddeley HS-125 that was taking former Congolese Prime Minister Moise Tshombé to the Congo from his exile in Spain, was hijacked over the Balearic Islands. The hijacker turned out to be Francis Bodenan, an agent of the Service de Documentation Extérieure et de Contre-Espionagge (SDECE), the French intelligence service, who diverted the aircraft to Algiers Airport, where Tshombé was immediately imprisoned.

For Black Jack Schramme, the event simply meant the end of the career of his financier and political protector, since the People's Democratic Republic of Algeria had signed an extradition treaty with the Democratic Republic of the Congo, where Tshombé had been sentenced to death on 13 March 1967. For this reason and to protect his own skin, on 5 July 1967, Schramme launched a surprise attack against the cities of Stanleyville, Kindú and Bukavú, starting the so-called Mercenaries Mutiny. Its objective was to overthrow the government of Lieutenant General Joseph-Désiré Mobutu, de facto president of the Congo since 1965 and to put Tshombé back in power. The rebellion resulted in four months of intense fighting, during which time the mercenaries were continuously supplied with weapons by the planes of Jack Malloch (another old Tshombé client). On 29 October 1967, Schramme's surviving mercenaries surrendered (or fled to Rwanda), with which Schramme and Malloch lost their chances of seeing Tshombé in power again, who ended up dead in his prison in Algiers on 29 June 1969.

The end of the parallel operations in the Congo allowed Malloch to concentrate all of his logistical resources in Biafra just as the secession war against Nigeria began to escalate in ferocity. For Nigerians, it was no longer just a question of achieving a military victory against Biafrans who had shown a total determination for independence, but of crushing that and any future attempt at rebellion on their territory, sending a clear message of power to all Western powers and to all the countries of the region.

From January 1968 onwards, the Nigerian siege began to generate a huge humanitarian disaster due to the systematic famine established in the areas populated by native Ibos; one of the tactics most used by the Nigerian forces was the sabotage of farmland so that the rebel soldiers (and their women and children) simply starved to death. The mercenaries operating against the Biafrans knew exactly what they were doing, to the point that one of them, a South African piloting a Soviet-made Ilyushin Il-28 bomber, openly called himself 'Genocide'.[5]

The brutality went so far as to completely choke the Biafran economy, to which end Nigeria decided to change its paper money overnight – which was the same used by the rebels – immediately stopping all transactions within the nascent Republic of Biafra. The rebels' response was not long in coming, in the form of the sabotage of the Nigerian economy consisting of the clandestine introduction of millions of bills, checks and bank notes (all false) through which they tried to generate inflation, devaluation of circulating currency

Following Biafra´s separation from Nigeria, on 30 May 1967, the nascent republic purchased three decommissioned Fouga CM.170 Magister training jets from the Austrian Air Force. The transfer from Graz to Lisbon took place in May 1968, in the Canadair CL-44D Swingtail, registration N604SA of Trans Mediterranean Airways, which would later become the LV-JZM of the Transporte Aéreo Rioplatense fleet. For the transfer of Magisters from Lisbon to são Tomé, the Biafrans turned to Jack Malloch, one of whose aircraft (L-1049 Super Constellation with registration 5T-TAC) can be seen in the background of this photograph. This registration was fake: the true 5T-TAC had crashed four months earlier (on 21 January 1968), near Port Harcourt, in Nigeria, killing all five on board. (Alex Rumley via Michael Draper via Malcom Porter)

and loss of purchasing power of Nigerian money with respect to Biafran money. To do this, tons of counterfeit money needed to enter Nigeria and this task could only be carried out efficiently by Jack Malloch's planes.

Malloch himself applied to carry out the clandestine flights, probably to prevent one of his pilots from disappearing with a plane loaded with money, which had already happened to another carrier who entrusted a former Congolese mercenary with the transfer of the shipment to Switzerland. This time things did not go well and while making a stopover for refuelling at the Lomé airport in Togo, Malloch and his co-pilot, the British Alister Wicks, were arrested with nine tons of Nigerian bank notes neatly arranged in the cargo hold of a Douglas DC-7F of the Affretair company (identified with the serial number 45463). Malloch and his crew were imprisoned, taken through the city as mercenaries and even put in front of a firing squad several times to confess to their part in the sabotage of Nigeria. Neither spoke and after six months in prison, both were released.

The only charge that the Togolese authorities could bring against Malloch was that the plane's registration had been tampered with, taking it from VP-WBO to ZP-WBO, thereby changing the nationality of the flag country, which was no longer blockaded Rhodesia but the distant Paraguay. The infraction weighed on the operating company, Affretair and not on the crew, so they were all acquitted. Fearing re-imprisonment, Malloch and Wicks disappeared immediately, leaving their plane stranded in Lomé, where it rusted to the side of the runway. Henceforth, Affretair's Douglas DC-7F also began to display identification numbers of the Rhodesian Air Force, with which they directly came to be considered military aircraft and therefore, unseisable. [6, 7]

Malloch's imprisonment did not stop arms supply flights to the Republic of Biafra, which his shell companies continued to carry out even during the months he was imprisoned. Jack's return to the arena made them stealthier and bolder, as if he wanted to outwit his captors and the Nigerian Army together. Night flights began to be carried out at low-altitude, always using different approach and escape routes, with the navigation lights turned off and with reduced engine power, so that even the blue flames typical of the exhaust pipes, could not be seen. Everything was done in absolute radio silence and foresightedly, every Air Trans Africa or Affretair plane was properly outfitted with a veritable combo of bogus documentation relating to the aircraft itself, crew and cargo. However, to Malloch's misfortune, the balance in Biafra began to tip to Nigeria's side.

In May 1969, the Biafrans launched a desperate offensive with the aim of maintaining the imbalance between the Nigerians and prolonging the existence of their breakaway nation as long as possible. They were supported by foreign mercenary pilots, who continued to send them food, medicine and weapons. One of the most notable, eccentric and sympathetic was the Swedish Count Carl Gustaf von Rosen, who led a puny air force of five small Malmö MFI-9 MiniCOINs armed with rocket launchers and machine guns in several attacks on the Nigerian military airfields of Port Harcourt,

Enugu, Benin and Ugheli, in the course of which he managed to hit some MiG-17 jets (used to attack Red Cross humanitarian aid planes) and three of the six Ilyushin Il-28 bombers used daily to hit the Biafran villages and farms. This was the swan song for the Biafran independentists, who finally collapsed after four years of famine and annihilation. The war ended on 15 January 1970, with the surrender of the last rebel strongholds in the town of Umuhaia. Until the last moment Jack Malloch supplied the defenders. [8]

No longer able to count on the succulent inflow of money that the illegal flights to Biafra had brought him, Malloch devoted his entire idle fleet to strengthening the never-interrupted clandestine airlift to and from Rhodesia. The goal was still to break the international blockade established in 1968 by the United Nations at the behest of Great Britain. To this end, in January 1970, he formed the freighter Air Gabon Cargo (based in Libreville, capital of the Gabonese Republic) and the passenger airline Afro Continental Airways (based in Salisbury, capital of Rhodesia). Both companies were, in reality, masquerades to continue covering up the pirate operations of Air Trans Africa and Affretair, whose planes rotated continuously between their inventories. In this way, no one knew exactly how many aircraft each company had at any given time, nor to what specific activities they were being applied by each one, since all the Douglas DC-7Fs were the same, they lacked paint schemes that could distinguish them and they did not have nationality marks or commercial signs. To make any trace even more difficult, Malloch used to hide the identity of each plane by covering its licence plates with paper and tape, thus completely fading his operations into the shadows.

The typical itinerary of Malloch's ghost planes can be perfectly seen with the Lockheed L-1049G Super Constellation serial 4685, the first four-engine with which Afro Continental Airways formally began operating. The plane was registered on 1 March 1967 with the Rhodesian registration VP-WAW as the property of Air Trans Africa, but it was transferred just two months later to Protea Airways (which on 12 May 1967 registered it in its name in South Africa as ZS-FAA). On 27 July 1967, the aircraft was re-registered as WP-WAW in the name of Air Trans Africa, which registered it as TR-LNY in the Gabon aircraft register in November 1968. The aircraft was finally registered in Rhodesia to Afro Continental Airways in July 1970, remaining with the registration WP-WAW until decommissioning in 1974. The aircraft is known to have been used actively during the Biafran War, being the last surviving of all Constellations and Super Constellations that Jack Malloch was losing through accidents, engine failures and landings in hostile countries in Africa, where several of them ended up seized.

Nominally, Afro Continental Airways had been organised as an airline and in October 1971, obtained formal authorisation from the Rhodesian government to provide non-scheduled charter passenger and cargo services plus a scheduled weekly service between Salisbury and Windhoek (then South-West Africa, today Namibia) and another weekly service between Salisbury and Lilongwe (then Nyasaland, today Malawi). In fact, the company functioned as a private feeder for the state-owned Air Rhodesia, but even so, it ended up making a loss since the international embargo made it commercially unviable. At that precise moment, the entire company became one of the many shell companies used by Malloch to mask the true owners. He was able to continue his anti-blockade flights to and from Rhodesia, arms smuggling and even supporting direct military operations, such as the drop of paratroopers over foreign countries carried out at a long-distance with the Super Constellation or the Douglas DC-7F that was circumstantially affected. Afro Continental Airways' income, which had been virtually nil with legal passenger traffic, skyrocketed with illegal arms trafficking, to the point that between 1977 and 1978 the company acquired the Boeing 707-430 four-engine jet serial 18056 (North American registration N9985F) with which he made innumerable flights to the United States, Europe and the East.[9, 10]

Unless they were required by the CIA, the SDECE, the Portuguese PIDE or the Israeli Mossad for covert operations, and in the absence of any regional conflict that demanded arms trafficking, from 1970 to 1979 Jack Malloch's planes were used primarily in the two-way airlift intended to circumvent the international blockade of Rhodesia. The operations included all of Malloch's airlines, plus a number of other land-based shell firms whose purpose was to complete the

The Lockheed L-1049G Super Constellation VP-WAW with which Jack Malloch capitalised Afro Continental Airways, one of the companies that carried out all kinds of illegal activities. (Robin Norton)

Afro Continental's Super Constellation seen taking-off from Salisbury International, with engine number three stalled, the least of the many irregularities committed by Malloch's pilots. (Robin Norton)

underground circuit. To offer an example, it is enough to consider the treatment given to the country's main export goods, such as beef, citrus fruits or beer; palletised meat was loaded at Salisbury Airport under false labels from Swazi producers and with equally false veterinary certificates issued by non-existent Swazi officials. The Rhodesian beer bore labels stating that it had been brewed in Botswana.[11]

In order to erase any connection to Rhodesia, most long-haul flights starting in Salisbury were planned to have a pre-stop in Libreville, from where the planes flew direct to Europe with shipping manifests doctored to make it appear as if the point of origin of the cargo was Gabon. The most used European destination was the Dutch city of Schiphol, near Amsterdam, where the Air Gabon Cargo company came to set up a permanent commercial office (which, as appropriate, channelled the demands to Affretair, Air Transport Africa or Afro Continental Airways). The office was located in the Freeport Cargo Building, opposite the Hilton Hotel, in whose suites both Malloch's crews and their business contacts stayed permanently. Arms purchases were not arranged at Schiphol, but at an office that had been established for this purpose in Geneva, Switzerland.[12]

The two-way airlift to Rhodesia not only saved the country from international economic suffocation, but also embarrassed the British government (which still refused to recognise the country's independence) and also the United Nations (whose isolation sanctions proved absolutely ineffective). In the context, Jack Malloch came to be considered a true patriot by his fellow Rhodesians (obviously the white-skinned ones), who owed him virtually everything that came into the country and the profits from almost everything that went out. The magnitude of his character reached such a level that in August 1973, the British newspaper *Sunday Times* dedicated the cover to him, exposing him as the main person responsible for sanction-busting and the breaking of the international blockade against his country. It was even discovered that the entire fleet engaged in the airlift was registered in Gabon, also exposing the pseudonym Malloch used for his illegal operations, which was not exactly 'Jack' but 'Tango Romeo', for TR – the civil registration prefix of that country.

For Malloch, accustomed to living in the shadows, the level of exposure was unwelcome but the end result was the opposite of what was claimed by the British press, as air operations began to take place more stealthily and more so, Malloch became the undisputed benchmark for any European, African or Asian businessman who wanted to transport anything by air to any part of the world secretly. The expansion of its operations to and from Rhodesia reached such a level that in May 1976, the British government took its third consecutive complaint to the United Nations regarding the breaking of the international blockade, citing Malloch as the main person responsible, who was referred to by first and last name in official English declarations.

The New York allegations brought Malloch's level of exposure to a dangerous point where he was liable to any type of international lawsuit or arrest warrant. The matter was profoundly serious, for Malloch's arrest would bring about the immediate collapse of his entire network of shell companies, simply because only he knew exactly the ins and outs of his operations. Thus, the Rhodesian government decided to grant him legal immunity, for which purpose it granted him military status by enrolling him as a reservist in the Rhodesian Air Force. The frame not only guaranteed him total impunity for the exercise of his anti-blockade flights, but also gave him an extra economic income as, from then onwards, his planes began to be openly used in direct military operations.

The first missions took place in January 1977, when Affretair/Air Transport Africa/Air Gabon Cargo Douglas DC-7Fs were used for very long-range parachute drops, to attack the groups' bases in Botswana, Mozambique and Zambia where communist guerrillas were infiltrating Rhodesia. That same month and in parallel, Malloch transferred the mercenary Bob Denard to Cotonou (Republic of Benin) where his soldiers of fortune launched a failed coup.[13]

To Malloch's concern, the insurgent groups began to rely on state-of-the-art Soviet weapons, including 9K32 Strela-2 passive infrared guidance portable anti-aircraft missiles (SA-7 'Gail' in NATO nomenclature). Using these, the militias of the Zimbabwe People's Revolutionary Army (ZIPRA) managed to shoot down two Air Rhodesia Vickers Viscount passenger planes, the first between Kariba and Salisbury on 3 September 1978 and the second on the reverse leg on 12 February 1979. Despite this, Douglas DC-7s were also used to generate noise screens over targets to prevent insurgents from discovering from which side Aérospatiale Alouette II assault helicopters or Rhodesian Air Force jets were coming to attack them, specifically the Thornhill-based Hawker Hunter FGA. Mk.9 and the New Sarum-based English Electric Canberra B. Mk2. On 23 November 1977 Malloch even used an Affretair Douglas DC-8 to divert Zimbabwe African National Liberation Army (ZANLA) insurgents 10 minutes before the air raid launched by Rhodesian forces on their main camp at Chimolo. For the white attackers, the mission was recorded simply as Operation Dingo, but for the blacks it went down in history as the 'Chimolo Massacre', since it resulted in 3,000 deaths and 5,000 wounded among ZANLA members, against the loss of only two members of the Rhodesian assault forces (a soldier and a pilot).

Thereafter, Malloch's pilots became bolder and more aggressive, operating virtually under the enemy's nose, as occurred in September 1979 during Operation Cheese in north-eastern Zambia. This was one of the last military actions deployed from Rhodesia, as on 21 September 1979 in London, delegations from the main parties in the conflict agreed to a truce, under the mediation of the British government. After a year, the black majority managed to vote for the first time in elections and the moderate Bishop Abel Muzorewa was elected Prime Minister. As a gesture of national unity, he baptised the country with the name of Zimbabwe-Rhodesia, agreeing to accept a provisional transition under the mandate of a British governor who was to call a general election the following year. Britain lifted all its sanctions on 12 December 1979 and the UN did the same four days later, immediately opening up international trade, especially with the neighbouring republics of Zambia, Mozambique, Tanzania, Angola, and Botswana. Fulfilling its commitment, on 18 April 1980, the British government recognised the independence of the new country, which was renamed the Republic of Zimbabwe.

The lifting of the international blockade marked the end of Jack Malloch's breakout flights, although it in no way meant the end of his undercover operations. It was impossible to escape the web of shadows after decades of association with politicians, mercenaries, traffickers and secret services. Rhodesia had been pacified but in 1980 the world was still at war in Afghanistan, Angola, Chad, Lebanon, Morocco, South Africa, Iran and Iraq. To meet the new demands for clandestine transport, Malloch relied on the combined capabilities of Afro Continental Airways (which already had a Boeing 707-430 cargo), Air Gabon Cargo (which had a Douglas DC-8F in its inventory) and the new CargOman Limited This company that had been established in 1976 in the city of Muscat, capital of the Sultanate of Oman, with commercial offices in Seeb, a relatively new town near the airport. CargOman was capitalised with a Douglas DC-8F twin to the one used by Air Gabon Cargo, both companies shared crews or contracts and when it was necessary not to expose them, both ceded the use of their aircraft to Afro Continental through aircraft utilisation contracts that were not always were registered in the records of the jurisdictions of operation. [14]

The CL-44 with registration LV-JTN seen while loading cattle at Campo Grande, in Brazil, while bound for Peru. (Mario Wolpi)

With this fleet of freighter jets at his disposal and with his vast experience in covert operations, it is not surprising that Jack Malloch was the first choice when the Israeli secret services decided to organise the logistics to carry out Operation Seashell, as only Malloch could ensure that the US weapons and parts that Israel was trading, reached Iran in absolute secrecy.

The transport of cattle was a frequent practice for the Canadair freighters of the TAR and its associated company Aerotransportes Entre Ríos. In this photograph, the first cow from a herd is lowered from the hold, down a specially installed chute of one of the Yukons. (Héctor Biondini)

However, all this fleet was not enough to meet the needs of the Israeli secret service, which gives an idea of the extraordinary volume of cargo that needed to be in Tehran at the highest possible speed. This being the case, Malloch decided to discreetly inquire which foreign company had one or more copies available. To do this, he placed his trust in Stuart Allan McCafferty, a 38-year-old Scotsman from Glasgow, who at that time declared his address at 70 Little Yeldham Road, Essex, Great Britain, although he had temporary residence in a rented apartment at 13962 S.S. 90th Avenue, Briarwoods District, Miami, Florida. McCafferty was a freight forwarder, aircraft broker and loadmaster qualified to transport all kinds of cargo on all types of cargo aircraft. Most importantly, he knew how to handle the papers, not only the air waybills and legal dispatches, but also the illegal ones so necessary for undercover or clandestine transport. Malloch was well aware of this ability as McCafferty had worked for him for six years at the Dutch Amsterdam-Schiphol airport as a supervisor of cargo operations for the Douglas DC-7F and DC-8F, Boeing 707 and Canadair CL-44 Swingtail aircraft that made up the combined fleets from Affretair, Air Trans Africa, Gabon Air Cargo and CargOman.[15]

At Jack Malloch's urging, McCafferty's first option was to contract the services of the English company Transmeridian Air Cargo. The choice seemed sensible considering it was a large freighter that operated seven Canadair CL-44s from Stansted Airport, located some 50km northeast of London, from where the ballast flight to Israel could be made without major costs. Thus, in June 1981, McCafferty contacted Mike Keegan, the owner of Transmeridian, from whom he requested a quote for the transfer of 360 tons of weapons to be shipped from Tel Aviv to Tehran. When the managers of the British cargo appraised the deal, they considered it too risky given that Iran was at war with Iraq, which could mean danger to the

George Batchelor, as seen on the cover of the Airline Executive magazine of December 1981. Miami's 'travel czar' had connections to Jack Malloch and US intelligence services, and thus acted as a liaison for contracting the Transporte Aéreo Rioplatense aircraft, in June 1981. (TBFINC)

aircraft and its crew. In order not to lose the possibility of obtaining some profit, Transmeridian, with George Batchelor on its board, proposed that the contract be entered into with the Argentine company TAR, to which, as mentioned earlier, it frequently referred contracts that it could not carry out, in exchange for a commission calculated on the final price charged to the customer.[16]

Fortunately for McCafferty, who was living in Miami, it turned out that one of the TAR planes, the Canadair CL-44D Swingtail registration LV-JTN, had been at the Miami International Airport since the first days of July 1981, as it had been brought there from Ezeiza so that the Rolls-Royce Tyne 515-10 engine serial number 7516 (position number two) was replaced by the Tyne serial number 5072. The works had been contracted with the firm Batch-Air Incorporated, owned by George Batchelor, in whose workshops the freighters of the Argentine company were frequently serviced.[17]

Of all the companies in the Batchelor Group, undoubtedly the most important were International Air Leases (through which had supplied aircraft and maintained commercial contact with more than 40 transport companies in the world) and Batch-Air, with which it had practically monopolised the service maintenance of them all. In fact, Batch-Air had the world's largest stock of Canadair CL-44 spare parts, making technical stopovers at its facilities a must for any Swingtail or Yukon freighter operator. In addition, George Batchelor personally knew Carlos Martínez Guerrero, president of TAR, as in May 1972, Batch-Air had mediated in the purchase of the Swingtail N604SA (future LV-JZM).

Through George Batchelor, McCafferty learned of the imminent availability of the CL-44D that was being serviced in Miami and also learned that TAR had experience operating to and from Iran

Armando Tola, co-founder of TAR, in the cockpit of the Boeing 707 with registration LV-MZE. (Oscar Bellini)

as by the end of 1979 it had made two successive flights to Tehran with Boeing 707 jets that had transported two shipments of Poxipol glue. When consulting with Jack Malloch (and the latter with the Israeli intelligence services), he learned that the Argentine company had already conducted sensitive transfers, including shipments of Argentine and Israeli arms to the governments of Nicaragua (under the dictatorship of Anastasio Somoza) and Panama (under the revolutionary government of Omar Torrijos).

The company's involvement as an arms carrier had come to light on 25 June 1977 when, en route from Portugal to Guatemala, one of its planes, the Canadair CL-44D registration LV-JZM under the command of Armando Tola and Marcelo De Gregorio, had to make a landing for refuelling on the island of Barbados, an English-speaking island state that had become independent from the United Kingdom just 11 years previously. Alerted by British intelligence, the Barbadian authorities commandeered the plane and confiscated 26 tons of Israeli 5.56 calibre weapons and ammunition. [18, 19, 20, 21]

6

DAZZLED BY THE PERSIAN GOLD

Having received the consent of the Israeli intelligence services, at the end of June or beginning of July 1981, McCafferty contacted a director of TAR in Miami, with whom he agreed to sign a charter agreement that would allow the transfer of cargo from Israel to Iran. In the document, signed in Miami on 7 July 1981, it was established that TAR would affect his freighter Canadair CL-44-D4 registration LV-JTN to perform a minimum of 100 flight hours during the period of 21 days between the 9 and 30 July 1981, for the purpose of transferring 'unrestricted ammunition and goods' between Ben Gurion Airports (Israel), Larnaca (Cyprus) and Tehran (Iran), and vice versa. Although the contract did not express it, the Larnaca-Tehran section could not be travelled directly but rather by flying over the territory of Turkey by airway. Notwithstanding this, McCafferty, as a charterer, undertook to 'obtain all the necessary transit rights for the fulfilment of the flights', forcing himself to deliver to the commander of the aircraft, before the departure of any flight, a copy of the corresponding take-off and landing permits. Given the international nature of the operation, the agreement expressly indicated that the flights would be carried out under the provisions of the Convention held on 12 October 1929 in the

TAR's second cargo jet, the Boeing 707 with registration LV-MZE (named 'San Jorge'), as seen on approach to Miami International, on 26 May 1982. (Gerard Helmer)

city of Warsaw, Poland, for the unification of certain rules relating to international air transport (Warsaw Convention), to which Argentina had adhered by Law No. 17,386 of 8 August 1967.[1]

The charter price was agreed in the sum of US$275,000, which included US$2,000 per flight hour for a minimum of 100 hours, plus US$75,000 for the transfer of the aircraft to Ben Gurion Airport. Against the signing of the contract, McCafferty paid $175,000 in cash, agreeing that the balance of $100,000 would also be paid in cash to the company's manager, Robert Harte, at the offices that Transportes Aéreos Rioplatenses had in Basel Airport, Switzerland. By special addition at the bottom of the contract, it was expressly established that the responsibility of the carrier was limited to delivering the aircraft, maintaining it and operating it during the term of the contract, fuel expenses, landing fees and operating costs being borne by the charterer of the flight and cargo handling. The latter made the agreed price a net profit for the cargo, because McCafferty as the charterer of the plane, was responsible for all its operating costs.

In the charter agreement, McCafferty stated that he would not allow the Transportes Aéreos Rioplatense plane to fly in contravention of any provision, regulation or law of government agencies or authorities that have jurisdiction over its operation as private transport, nor would he allow the aircraft to be used for the transportation of cargo based on third-party leases. McCafferty was also responsible for delivering the cargo packed in accordance with IATA regulations for the carriage of restricted items. (Both demonstrations, of course, were not faithful, considering the nature of the flights inherent in Operation Seashell.)

Regarding insurance, the charter agreement provided that McCafferty would take out coverage for the hull in the amount of $1,500,000 obliging himself to prevent the plane from flying outside the geographical limits established in the policy. Since Iran was at war, the insurance was contracted directly at Lloyd's of London, declaring to the insurer that the cargo would be made up of 'agricultural material and other equipment'. For the highest risk section, between Cyprus and Tehran, coverage equivalent to 110 percent of the value of the aircraft and cargo was contracted.

McCafferty accepted to include in the contract the declaration of TAR, according to which, the company was not responsible for the loss, damages or delays that were resulting from any act, negligence or omission on the part of the commander of the aircraft or its crew, nor acts of war. He also accepted that, in the event of a lawsuit or claim, the jurisdiction would be extended to the Federal Courts of the City of Buenos Aires. The signature of the TAR representative on the contract signed with McCafferty is illegible and not clear. Two sources consulted specify that it was the signature of José María Patetta, General Manager of the company.[2, 3]

Once the terms of the contract were agreed, José María Patetta proceeded to convene the crews that would have to comply with the flights to Tehran. To his surprise, many of the TAR commanders did not accept the call, arguing the danger of carrying 'special cargo' in the Middle East was too great. The most experienced even dared to express that it was crazy to bring weapons with a civilian company to a country that was officially at war. The crews, therefore, were made up of those most in need of extra payment. They were Commander Héctor Ismael Cordero Jaureguiberry, co-pilots José López Beltrán and Hermete Mateo Santiago Boasso; and the aeronautical technicians Lucas Varela, Roberto Melo and José Raúl Burgueño. Oscar Palacio was proposed to stow the cargo, although his presence did not seem necessary since Stuart McCafferty would participate in all flights as loadmaster.[4]

The composition of the team was unusual to say the least, since there was only one commander and one loader for the 12 flights, which were expected to be carried out continuously. This meant a significant effort based on cumulative fatigue of the crossings, which would be made in a west-east direction and vice versa, cutting meridians and time zones which has an impact on the circadian rhythm of the human body. However, the economic stimulus was important (especially for Cordero, who would perform all the flights) and for the rest, the crews of TAR, were not precisely characterised by complying with the minimum rest times and maximum service times provided for in the Resolution 571/68 of the Commander-in-Chief of the Argentine Air Force as the work of a freighter was essentially unpredictable. To give an example of the recruitment, the co-pilot Hermete Boasso was already retired when he received the call from Patetta, despite which he agreed to join the crew to provide himself with an extra income.[5]

In order to completely conceal the identity of the company that owned the plane and so that TAR could never be linked to the cargo or the itineraries, Jack Malloch proposed that the entire operation

The soul of the Transporte Aéreo Rioplatense were the technicians who provided maintenance to its aircrafts in the most diverse and often extreme conditions. The "oilers", as they were affectionally called by the pilots, never left any CL-44s on the ground, despite the chronic shortage of parts.

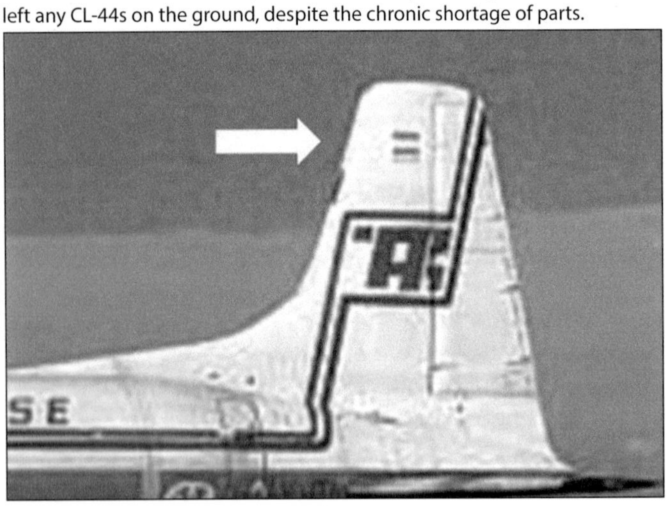

In July 1981, at Ezeiza, the 'oilers' refused to erase the Argentine flag from the fin of the LV-JTN, although being instructed to conceal the identity of the aircraft prior to its trip to Israel. (Héctor Biondini)

be carried out under the cover of Afro Continental Airways. It was the company named in all shipping documents, flight plan forms and international overflight permits over Israel, Cyprus, the Turkish Republic of Cyprus, Turkey and Iran, that were to be issued. In this way, Afro Continental became the front to celebrate the transport contracts inherent to Operation Seashell, which were signed with the Israeli company Elul Company, owned by David Kolitz. Under this scheme, McCafferty acted as charterer for the company that was to carry out the flights and TAR simply became the actual carrier.

In addition, Jack Malloch (or the Mossad) demanded that the Argentine flags on the upper part of the empennage be removed from the plane, as well as the Argentine legend inscribed immediately below along with all commercial signs. It was an old practice for smugglers to hide the origin of their devices since, in the latitudes through which they would have to operate, it would be very difficult to deduce the nationality of the plane from the first two letters of its registration (LV-). The order to erase the flags was given when Canadair was still in Buenos Aires, but the mechanics at the maintenance shop that TAR had at the Ezeiza airport, flatly refused to carry out this task. This was partly out of national pride and partly because, according to a navigators' tradition (inherited by aero-navigators), leaving a ship without a flag or erasing the name on it brings bad luck, since it simply means leaving it without identity, without essence, without soul.[6]

Thus, the LV-JTN left Argentina with its flags and nationality signs intact and with the company's trade name still painted on both sides of the fuselage. However, upon arriving in Miami, the story changed completely. On 6 July 1981, while the work to replace the number two engine was being completed, the Batch-Air operators mounted a hydraulic stepladder, reached the top of the plane's tail and covered the two hand-painted flags on each side, as well as the word Argentina that was immediately below. It is highly probable that the flag and the letters had not been sanded, since it would have been quite difficult to paint them again days later in the same place. This suggests that they were covered with paper or white adhesive tape, the colour of which quickly blended in with the white paint on the glue. However, the fuselage was sanded down to eradicate the legend of Transporte Aéreo Rioplatense on both sides. They obviously lacked time, because they could only complete the work on the left side, that is, the side with the doors.[7]

With partially erased trademarks, no flags and a new engine just assembled, on 7 July 1981 the Canadair CL-44 registration LV-JTN left Miami International Airport to begin a 7,445km transatlantic jump to Amsterdam-Schiphol, the Netherlands, where a night stopover was planned to rest the crew. Taking advantage of the fact that the plane's hold was completely empty, Stuart McCafferty loaded a Jeep CJ-7 into it (here known as Ford 4X4 Potro), to be used at the destination.

Everything seemed normal until, upon arriving at Amsterdam-Schiphol, several agents of the Korps Nationale Politie, the Dutch national police in charge of airport control, appeared and began to insistently ask about the cargo on the plane. The airport authorities had apparently received an anonymous message informing them that the Argentine cargo ship was transporting arms and the agents were determined to discover the contraband and its circumstances. However, when accessing the Canadair cargo hold, they only found McCafferty's own Jeep, which was disembarked at the airport itself.

It is not clear who leaked the information regarding the movement of the Argentine freighter, since Operation Seashell was a secret kept under seven locks. The infidelity could have come from one of the shady underworld characters in which McCafferty moved, or from some resentful arms merchant for not having been summoned to the business. As it was (and the speculations can be endless) the truth is that the Dutch police were already aware that the CL-44 Swingtail registered LV-JTN could be involved in something strange and if the Dutch knew about it, naturally the Western intelligence services would also know about it, since they were all members of INTERPOL, the International Criminal Police Organisation, which at that time was very active in preventing the trafficking of arms that could supply every country. Increasingly this was the virulent Middle and Far Eastern terrorist groups, notably the Palestine Liberation Organisation (PLO), the Al-Fatah Organisation, Palestinian Islamic Jihad, the Popular Front for the Liberation of Palestine (PFLP), the Democratic Front for the Liberation of Palestine (FDLP), the Front for the Liberation of Palestine (FLP), the National Council of Resistance of Iran and the Organisation of the People's Mujahideen of Iran.[8]

On the night of 10 July 1981, when the Canadair de TAR was authorised to take off from the Amsterdam-Schiphol Airport, the Israeli intelligence services already knew that Operation Seashell

During the inspection of the wreckage of the CL-44 in Armenia, Commodore Rodolfo Echegoyen found the drift rudder intact, together with the Argentine flag, but without the title 'Argentina' immediately below. This find was puzzling, because the aircraft flew from Miami to Israel with its nationality markings covered, as shown on this photograph taken at Amsterdam-Schipol, on 7 July 1981. The only possible explanation is that the Argentine flag was discovered or repainted in Israel – which is rather unlikely. (Peter de Groot)

could be revealed. However, the logistical machinery was already in motion and could not be stopped, mainly because commitments made to the Iranians, who had already paid for the weapons they needed, had to be honoured. That being the case, it was imperative to quickly cover-up the identity of the Argentine freighter, so that its movement to and from Tehran could not be tracked by the intelligence and security services. In order to dispel the identity of the plane, Jack Malloch proposed omitting the use of its Argentine civil registration in radio communications with the air traffic services of all the countries that were going to be flown over. This was, the plane would not be identified as LV -JTN but only by the flight code granted by Israel and Iran to the company Afro Continental Airways for the outbound (KY223) and return (YR224) legs. These codes were fake. The company to which the 'KY' code was assigned in 1981 has not been identified, but according to the IATA nomenclator, the 'YR' code corresponded to Grand Canyon Airlines, a non-scheduled flight company. which since 1936 operated from the Boulder City airport, Nevada, United States.[9, 10]

The plane landed at the 'Ben Gurion' Airport in Lod, Israel, at five in the morning on 10 July 1981. Once on the ground, it was not directed to the commercial platform, in front of the passenger terminal, but to the military sector, located exactly at the other end of the airfield. Knowing that they would have to meet face-to-face with the applicants for the transportation service, all the Argentines were impeccably dressed in the company's uniform, consisting of a black suit with gold trim and matching cap, white shirt, black lace-up shoes and some beautiful silver wings on the right side of the sack. However, there was no formality to receive them, nor did their arrival have the solemnity they would have expected.

As soon as filming stopped, the turbines turned off and the access door opened, the plane was boarded by Mossad agents who entered by a ladder. Without further introductions, they searched the cabin, Compartment B and the cargo hold, where they found absolutely nothing since McCafferty's vehicle had remained in Amsterdam. The Israeli agents promptly seized the personal documents of all the Argentines, probably a measure of indirect control, since none of them could leave Israel without the prior authorisation and knowledge of the secret service. They were then loaded into various vehicles and taken to the Dan Accadia Hotel, located at 122 Ramat Yam Avenue, Hertsliya, facing the Mediterranean Sea. The hotel itself was a true resort, but it escaped no one that in the days to come it would be something of a gilded cage, so isolated from the airport and the city of Tel Aviv that it would never be visited by a crew member. no airline, so no one could notice the presence of the Argentines. [11]

While the entire Argentine contingent settled into the rooms of the Dan Accadia, Stuart McCafferty applied himself to preparing the first dispatch to Iran. As a safeguard for that flight, which would be exploratory, the Israelis proposed that the cargo be made up of seven tons of nursing equipment, plus parts and components easily identifiable as civilian use. It was a prudent way of keeping safe the true nature of the entire operation if something went wrong on the most critical segment of the first contracted circuit – the stopover in Cyprus. Consequently, various innocent hospital materials, F-4 Phantom II fighter-bomber tyres (which could perfectly pass as rubber tyres for the wheels of any vehicle), M-60 tank engine parts and M-113 (which could pass for innocuous spare parts) and replacement guns for M-48 tanks (which could pass perfectly for tubes or cylinders for the oil industry) were suggested. The contracts were carefully drafted to appear absolutely innocent. The 'tubes, cylinders and spare parts' were officially sent to a German company that unsurprisingly, did not exist.[12]

Under strict secrecy and away from the prying eyes of any curious person, the LV-JTN was loaded by Israeli soldiers during the night of 11–12 July 1981. The crew for the first flight to Iran was made up of Ismael Cordero (commander), José López Beltrán (co-pilot) and Lucas Varela (on board mechanic). The three Argentines would be accompanied by Stuart McCafferty, who would fulfil the functions of loadmaster, which in this case meant only handling the necessary papers to achieve the cover-up at the planned stopover, Larnaca International Airport, on the island of Cyprus. To this end, he carried a set of documents showing that the plane was flying empty. In the words of Malcolm Porter, Jack Malloch's loadmaster:

> This was, of course, one of the oldest and most tried methods of avoiding getting caught by customs. In the event that, after landing, the aircraft was inspected by Cypriot customs, the original documents would be changed to show that the cargo had arrived at its declared destination and would therefore be disembarked. [13]

Given the latter assumption, experience taught McCafferty that customs officials around the world were more concerned with paperwork than with effective control of shipments. Therefore, it was foreseeable that once the papers were verified, they would not stay to witness the eventual unloading, especially when delays were forced or misunderstandings were invented. Most likely, after checking the clearance papers, the customs officers would remain in their offices, after which the plane could present an exit permit with newly forged documents to record that it had been loaded in Cyprus and not Israel. In the case of the first flight to Tehran, all these provisions even seemed unnecessary, as the plane would be loaded with material that could easily be presented as civilian use in the event of a hold inspection. In such a case, the documents indicating that the plane was flying empty could be quickly exchanged for ones that adequately detailed the 'civilian' cargo. Obviously, the manifest that indicated that the plane was flying empty would be the first document to be delivered to the Cypriot customs officers, discreetly accompanied by a succulent tip so that they simply signed and did not come close to verifying.

One of the last photographs of the Canadair CL-44 coded LV-JTN, from 9 July 1981, taken on the parking platform of Amsterdam-Schipol International. Although the image is deliberately bad, it is illustrative of a relevant detail: the Argentine flag and the title placed near the top of the fin have been erased – or covered. In other words, the aircraft left Miami without nationality markings, as a part of the cover-up for flights it would have to carry out within Operation Seashell. (Oscar Palace)

Fully loaded with 'civil use equipment', the Canadair de TAR took off for the first time towards Cyprus at midnight on 11 July 1981, with the stated purpose of refuelling before continuing the flight to Iran using the airways that passed over Turkey. To McCafferty's surprise, as soon as the freighter's wheels touched Larnaca International Airport, the crew was informed that the plane would be boarded by Cypriot customs officers. The officials not only exhaustively verified the papers, but also the shipment, which clearly showed that they had been previously informed by the security and intelligence services, most likely INTERPOL.

As they found that only medical items, pipes, tyres and spare parts destined for a German company were being transported in the hold (all of which matched one of the forged sets of papers), the customs officers quickly released the plane, which was authorised to refuel and proceed to Tehran. For McCafferty, who was used to moving in the shadows, this second exposure was particularly uncomfortable. Not only because it hindered the business (the 'civilian equipment' alibi had come out perfectly) but because Cyprus was a veritable nest of spies. If Cypriot customs officers were on alert, it was almost certain that the true nature of the flights would already be known to the Turks, the British and the Americans, for their agents were everywhere.

There was not long to wait as the Russians had already been monitoring the increase in flights that was being generated in Israel. In fact, the Soviet Union's air defence radars had detected an unusual movement of planes flying from Israel to Iran bordering the southern Soviet Republics of Armenia and Azerbaijan, which suggests that Operation Seashell had summoned many more planes from many more cargo companies. This may explain the anonymous tip received by Dutch National Police officers at Amsterdam Airport Schiphol and even the zeal of Cypriot customs officers at Larnaca Airport, as both may have been tipped off by more than the usual sources.

The Soviets were particularly susceptible to air movements near their borders as they were genuinely concerned with preventing a surprise NATO nuclear attack on their cities, whether carried out with conventional bombers or Inter Continental Ballistic Missiles (ICBMs). The state of permanent radar surveillance, the continuous collection of data and the constant fear of not being caught off guard can only be explained by the state of paranoia that characterised the military leadership of the two superpowers in conflict during the Cold War.

To make matters worse, the southern border of the Soviet Union, especially the political border of the Soviet Republics of Armenia and Azerbaijan with Turkey and Iran, had been the scene of a notable increase in provocation and attrition flights organised by the Central Intelligence Agency (CIA) and the United States Department of Defense. The penetration flights over Soviet territory had begun in the late 1950s with clear espionage purposes and a large part of them had been carried out from Persian air bases during the reign of the Shah of Iran. Taking advantage of the paranoia of the Russians and with the purpose of keeping them under continuous pressure that would increase their war expenses (and, in parallel, wear out their domestic economy), in February 1981 the United States began to launch against the Soviet Union what the Pentagon called 'psychological operations', or PSYOPS.[14]

The psychological operations gave the expected result as they were accompanied by the bellicose rhetoric of President Ronald Reagan, the increase in US military exercises near the Soviet borders and an effective increase in the US capacity to thwart the early warning systems of its counterpart. In May 1981, Yuri Andropov, the head of the Soviet intelligence headquarters, the KGB, announced to his closest group of officers that the United States was actively preparing for war and warned them of 'the certain possibility of a first nuclear strike.' Based on this concept, all the efforts of the external agents of the KGB were channelled towards the detection and evaluation of signals that revealed the preparation of a surprise nuclear attack, not only in the military sphere but also in the political and economic sectors, defence civil and related sectors.[15]

As can be seen, the flights that Canadair de TAR had already begun to carry out were taking place in an area under intense surveillance from both sides of the border, since the scans of the Soviet radar network in Armenia and Azerbaijan overlapped with the NATO radar network set up in Turkey and Cyprus. They all

The lineage of the Transporte Aéreo Rioplatense can be traced back to 1957, when Transcontinental SA was founded, a company aiming to satisfy customers from the private sector, who demanded services not provided by the state-owned Aerolinas Argentinas. The Transcontinental operated this Curtiss C-46 Commando and two Bristol Britannias, but its story ended with bankruptcy in 1961: this traumatic experience drove one of its technicians, Edgardo Luzzi, and pilots Ernesto Wood and Emilio González Bonorino, into establishing a new air freighting enterprise. The new born company, Aerotransportes Entre Ríos, operated the old C-46 registered LV-FTO, saved from Transcontinental. (Artwork by Luca Canossa)

As soon as the judge ruling the bankruptcy of Transcontinental SA permitted them, Luzzi and friends assumed control over the Curtiss C-46A-41-CU with registration LV-FTR. By this time, the aircraft was already converted into the civilian CW-20T airliner, but Luzzi's team then re-built it into a pure freighter using the cargo doors, landing gear, fin and rudder from the C-46 with registration CX-AYI that crashed in San Luis. Once ready to pay for proceeds and wearing the full livery of the newly-established Aerotransportes Entre Rios, it looked like the image shown. (Artwork by Luca Canossa)

The Bristol Type 175 Britannia emerged in the late 1940s on requirement from the British Overseas Airways Corporation (BOAC), as a medium-to-long-range airliner. A highly-promising design that was delayed by wrangling between the Ministry of Supply and BOAC over research and development costs, and engine-related problems, it was certified for service only in 1955, by then the market was swept by pure jet airliners and most of the 85 examples built were soon converted into air freighters. Aerotransporte Entre Rios began operating the type in 1967–1968, when it leased this example – registered as LV-JNL – from Batch Air, a company owned by George Batchelor. It served with the Aerotransportes Entre Rios until 12 July 1970, when written off in an accident at Ezeiza International. (Artwork by Goran Sudar)

Based on Bristol Britannia, the Canadair CL-44 was developed and manufactured in the late 1950s and 1960s. A total of only 39 were built, of which the Royal Canadian Air Force (RCAF) acquired 12 under the designation CC-106 Yukon and pressed them into service starting in 1961. Due to the chronic shortage of spare parts – a result of the type never entering large-scale production – all CC-106 Yukons were retired from military service by 1970. On advice from Batchelor and with financial support of several investors from the USA, four were acquired by Aerotransportes Entre Rios: the first of them – officially handed over on 13 November 1970 – wore the registration LV-JSY. (Artwork by Goran Sudar)

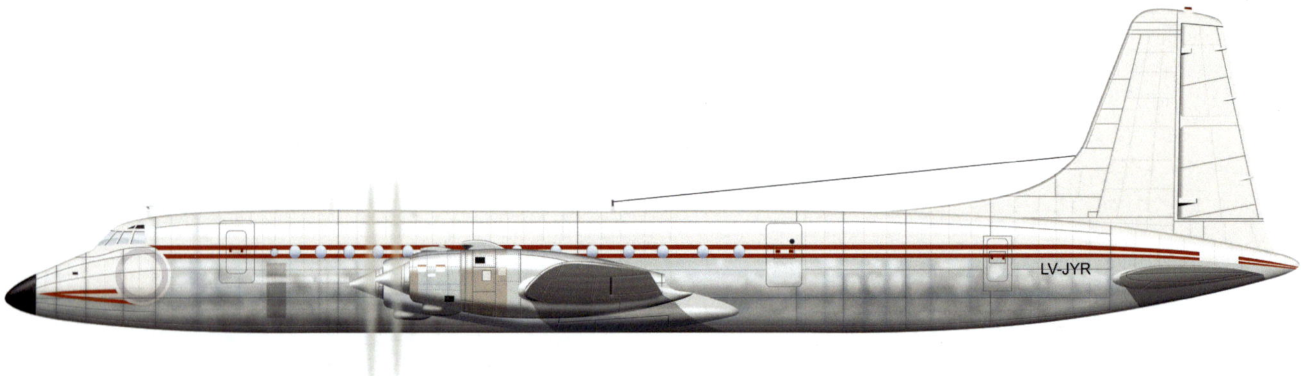

Once initial problems were resolved, the CL-44 proved highly efficient and dependable in service. Between others, it held the world record for its class by flying 10,860km (6,750nm) from Tokyo to RCAF Station Trenton, in Ontario, in 17 hours and 3 minutes, at an average speed of 640km/h (400mph). Another Yukon later remained airborne for 23 hours and 51 minutes (both records were bettered only by the Boeing 747, over a decade later). The second Yukon leased by Aerotransportes Entre Rios, wore the registration LV-JYR. It arrived in Argentina in November 1971, wearing the livery shown here: with RCAF markings removed, but still retaining some traces of them, including the two red cheat lines down the fuselage. (Artwork by Goran Sudar)

Aiming to further improve its services, in early 1971, the Aerotransportes Entre Rios – meanwhile in the process of being reorganised as the Transporte Aéreo Rioplatense – leased its first CL-44D4 Yukon from Batch Air: the aircraft with construction number 34, and the US registration N605SA. Nicknamed the Swingtail, the CL-44D4 was unique in having its entire tail section hinged: this could be opened using hydraulic actuators to load large items quickly. An inflatable seal at the hinge-break enabled the maintenance of the cabin pressure, and eight hydraulic-operated locks ascertained structural integrity. In service with the TAR, this aircraft received the registration LV-JTN. Usually, the 'Juliet Tango November' had the Argentine flag and title ´Argentina´ applied high on its fin: when it became involved in Operation Seashell, these were removed (or covered), as shown in insert. (Artwork by Goran Sudar)

The reforms of the Khrushchev-era reduced the Soviet armed forces and pilot training to the degree where they were severely felt when, in the early 1970s, Sukhoi Su-15 interceptors were introduced into service. The shortage of pilots and Sukhoi Su-15UT two-seat conversion trainers was such that when the 166th Guards Fighter Aviation Regiment of the Soviet Air Defence Force (V-PVO) was ordered to convert to the new type, in 1970, it had only enough pilots for two squadrons, and they had to use MiG-15UTIs and Sukhoi Su-7Us for training. This was one of 166th Guards Fighter Aviation Regiment's early Su-15 interceptors, and it is shown with that version's original radome and its sole armament: one R-98 air-to-air missile installed under each wing. (Artwork by Tom Cooper)

The 166th's third squadron was entirely staffed by pilots drafted from the Volunteer Society for Cooperation with the Army, Aviation and Navy (DOSAAF). They completed their conversion at Krasnovodsk AB, in 1973, but the regiment was declared operational only two years later, while deployed at Sandar AB, outside Marneuli, in the Soviet Republic of Georgia. By then, it began receiving improved Su-15TM interceptors. Even then, the armament of this variant was still limited to a pair of R-98 air-to-air missiles. This jet, 'Red 30' was the Su-15TM flown by Captain Valentin Kulyapin during the fateful intercept that resulted in him ramming the Canadair CL-44D coded LV-JTN of the Transporte Aéreo Rioplatense, on 18 July 1981. (Artwork by Tom Cooper)

In the aftermath of Kulyapin's experience, but also that of several other intercepts of Western aircraft that ventured into the Soviet airspace of the late 1970s and early 1980s, in 1981 the V-PVO ordered its Su-15TMs to be upgraded through the addition of UPK-23-250 gun pods with twin-barrel 23mm cannons under the fuselage. Later on, also APU-60-I rails for R-60M short-range air-to-air missiles (ASCC/NATO-codename 'AA-8 Aphid') were added under the inboard section of the leading edge of each wing. Thus came into being, the 'ultimate' form of the Su-15TM, as best-known in the West ever since, and illustrated here, on another jet of the 166th Guards Fighter Aviation Regiment, V-PVO. (Artwork by Tom Cooper)

Lockheed L-1049H Super Constellation with registration LV-JJO of Aerotransportes Entre Rios, as seen at Miami in December 1968. The aircraft still had no AER logo, but it already wore the temporary registration LV-PKW, used for its transfer to Argentina. (Marcelo W. Miranda)

A Super Constellation of the Afro-Continental Airways, as seen without any company markings at Mount Hampden airfield, outside Salisbury, in Rhodesia (nowadays Zimbabwe), in 1974. The continuous dodging and changing of identities of this aircraft was a hallmark of Jack Malloch. (Chris Knagg)

The Douglas DC-8-55(F) freighter with the registration A4O-PA, of CargOman, the last company established by Jack Malloch, on the apron of Amsterdam-Schipol International, in February 1981. Available information indicates that this aircraft was also used for clandestine flights to Iran. (Peter de Groot)

The Canadair CL-44D4-6 Swingtail registration LV-JTN of Transporte Aéreo Rioplatense photographed on 7 July 1981 upon arrival at Amsterdam-Schipol Airport, the Netherlands. That day his crew was detained by the Korps Nationale Politie, in order to find out the purpose of his trip to the Middle East. Obviously, they were already informed that the plane would be used to transport weapons. (Photo: Peter de Groot)

Loading of the LV-JTN with help of a forklift. This is how it must have looked while being loaded with spares for the Iranian armed forces, at the Lod/Ben Gurion International, in Israel. (Hector Biondini)

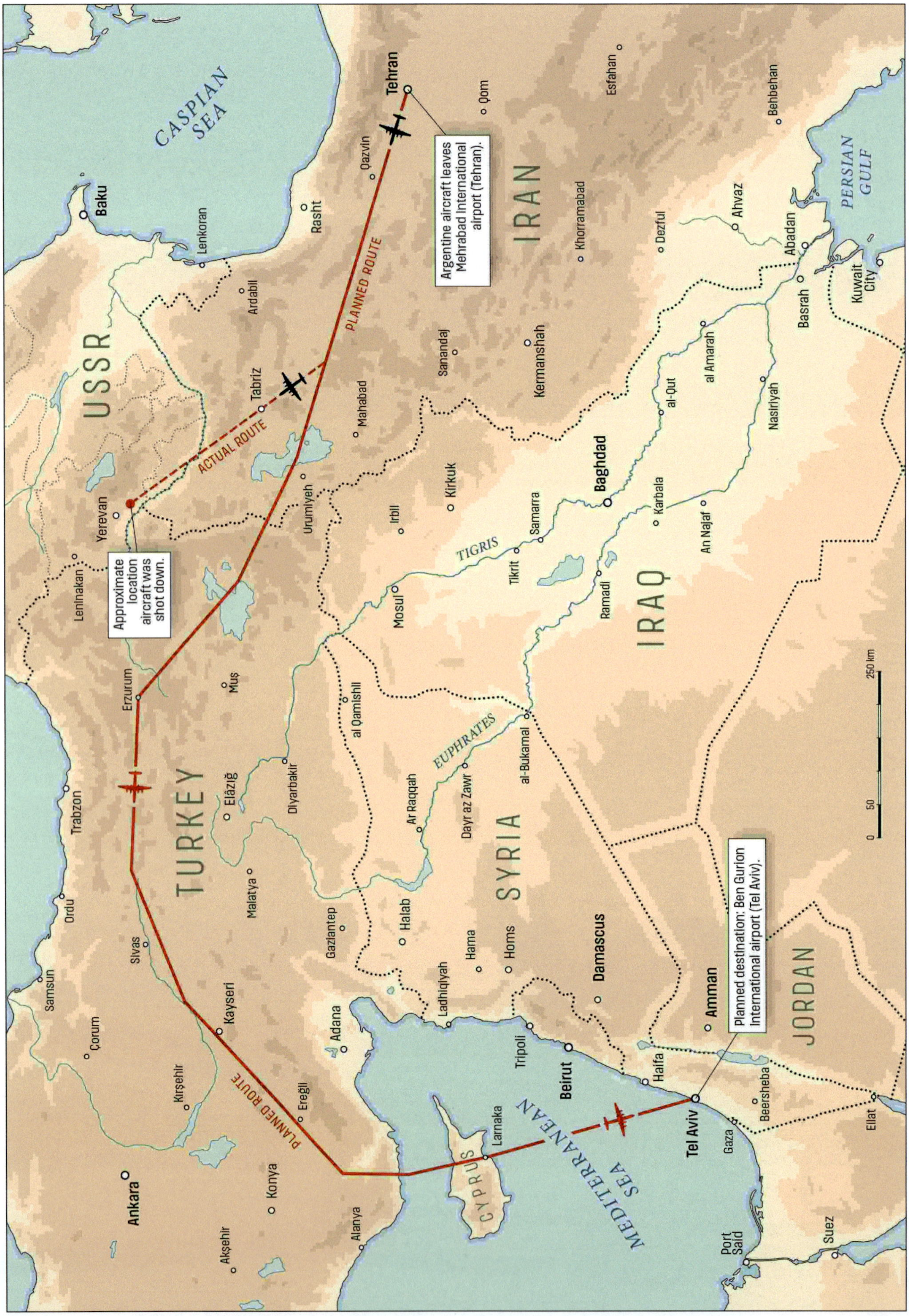

A map of the flight of the CL-44D4 Yukon with registration LV-JTN from 18 July 1981. The full line denotes the planned route, from Mehrabad International, via Turkey and Cyprus (without a stop) to Ben Gurion International, in Israel. The dotted line denotes the actual route that took it into the Soviet airspace. (Map by Micky Hewitt)

The last-ever photograph of the Canadair CL-44 Swingtail with registration LV-JTN, this time taken during the departure from Amsterdam-Schipol International, on 10 July 1981, after being released by the Dutch National Police. Multiple Western intelligence services were already aware that the aircraft was involved in some kind of a secret operation in the Middle East. (Rob Jonker)

monitored the entire airspace, but in particular to check civil aircraft did not stray one millimetre from commercial airways. Air navigation charts expressly indicated that in Turkey, Iran and the Soviet Union, flying outside the airways where air traffic services were provided was strictly prohibited.[16]

Despite the disturbing customs inspection in Cyprus, the truth is that the first flight to Tehran went ahead as planned. The navigation went smoothly, the cargo was delivered as arranged, the interested parties were satisfied with the dispatch and the entire crew was able to prove to themselves that a long-distance operation such as the one that had been contracted, towards a country at war, did not really seem that risky. The TAR CL-44 returned to Tel Aviv reversing the route it had taken to reach Tehran and, by sunset on 12 July1981, it was parked again on the military platform of the Ben Gurion International.

The second flight of the Canadair CL-44 of TAR to Tehran took place on 14 July 1981. All the 'real' dispatch documents that had to be carried on board were forged, while the real ones were impossible to understand because they were encrypted. The Israeli intelligence service had compiled a painstaking list of simple code names based on numbers for each component or reference to Operation Seashell. So, for example, a Rafael Shafrir air-to-air missile was simply '1', a Howitzer gun was '2', an UZI machine gun was '8', and the destination Iran was '11'. In the encrypted papers, the Argentine plane had the code name 'Britannia', evidently because of the similarity between the Canadair CL-44D Swingtail and its direct predecessor, the Bristol 175 Britannia, a very familiar model for the Israelis since it had been part of the commercial fleet of the airline El Al Israel.[17]

The second flight from Tel Aviv to Iran was direct, without a stopover in Larnaca or any other airport. It is highly possible that the plane followed exactly the same airways, flying over Cyprus but not landing, thus distancing its presence on the island. In such a case, the forged papers would only have been useful in the event of having to make a technical stopover at an alternative airport, although this time the load was compromising, as Oscar Palacio, the loadmaster sent by TAR, was able to see 'boxes and boxes of cannonballs', that is, artillery shells. As this time the operation was carried out in daylight during all the legs, from the air they were able to observe the main geographical landmarks: the rugged relief of the great Turkish plateau, the enormous Van and Urumiye lakes, the characteristic aridity of almost all Iranian surface.

The landing and subsequent unloading in Tehran were done quite quickly and without any inconvenience. The return trip to Israel took place the same day and included a stopover to refuel at Larnaca Airport, which was completely innocuous as, in the event of a new review, Cypriot customs or security agents would find a completely empty warehouse. Thus, from the point of view of secrecy, the second operation to Iran was impeccable, because the plane did not touch Cyprus on the way out, but on the way back, when it was already flying in ballast. However, by the time Canadair shut down its engines on the apron of Ben Gurion Airport, the Israelis were certainly worried. That same 14 July 1981 in the afternoon, while the plane was completing its final leg to Tel Aviv, journalist Dan Rather, host of the evening news programme on the American television channel CBS, had released the following information on the air: 'CBS is aware from credible sources that the Israeli government is supplying weapons to Iran through third parties. The weapons are dispatched to a neutral airport, from which they are transferred to their final destination in Tehran'.[18]

The news was bad, as it was clear that someone had leaked details of Operation Seashell to the press. However, the imprecision of the journalistic report suggested the source of the information had been the Soviet intelligence services, which could only infer the type of cargo from the origin and frequency of each plane they saw taking off from Israel on their radars.

Pre-emptively, the Mossad decided to distance from the operation. Intelligence services are not known for being daring (on the contrary, they are extremely cautious) and the Jews knew they were playing with fire. For this reason, the third flight was scheduled for Friday, 17 July 1981.

7

INTO THE SOVIET JAWS

On 17 July 1981 at night, the Canadair CL-44 was just over the Ararat system. Given its secret mission, in radio traffic it was not identified with its Argentine civilian registration LV-JTN, but with the flight number KY223 that had been given to the company Afro Continental Airways – one of the masquerades under which were the air transfers of weapons inherent to Operation Seashell. To the surprise of the radar operators of the Soviet defence system, who were continuously monitoring the border between Armenia and Turkey, in order to fly over the Ararat mountains, the plane left the airway it was flying through, which was highly suspicious given that the flight outside the routes controlled by air traffic services, was prohibited in

Turkey. To make matters worse, immediately afterwards, the plane entered the airspace of the Soviet Union without permission, where flying outside the airway was also prohibited.[1]

It is not clear why Commander Héctor Cordero passed over the Ararat system, since the flight over Turkish airspace was not free. It is likely that he did it simply to mark the point for geographical reference. Given its size and the way in which it emerges in the middle of a plain, the Ararat system constitutes an inescapable visual reference in flight, since its high snowy peaks can be seen perfectly in the distance, even at night, as the snow shines by the light of the moon. In the air navigation charts in force in 1981 (and in the current ones) the peaks were relatively close to IGDIR, which was an en-route air reporting point located over the Turkish city of Iğdir. For any pilot who reach the IGDIR position was very simple to orientate towards Tehran. The issue was that the IGDIR position was the last reporting point of the airway that led to Yerevan, in the Soviet Republic of Armenia. There was no airway leading from IGDIR reporting point to Iranian airspace. That put the Soviets on alert, even more so when they saw that the echo registered on their radar screens entered their own territory. Only a military plane could move outside the airway, so they assumed that it was an electronic intelligence plane, that is, a spy plane.

The Soviet defence recorded a large number of air intrusions over the Armenian-Azerbaijani border from Turkey and Iran, many of which had ended in the downing of the raiders. The episodes dated back to the very beginning of the Cold War and had escalated in intensity ever since, the daring of the raiders being matched only by the determination of the defenders to bring them down. The first case occurred on 27 August 1953, when a British Royal Air Force English Electric Canberra bomber, modified for photographic reconnaissance, was intercepted by a MiG-15 fighter over the Kasputin Yar missile launch range, the Soviet cosmodrome located between the cities of Volgograd and Astrakhan. Russian pilot Mikhail Shulga scored cannon hits on the Canberra, which continued to fly until it exited Soviet airspace and landed at an Iranian airfield.[2]

The first case of a shoot-down occurred five years later, on 27 June 1958, when a four-engine Douglas C-118 Liftmaster freighter of the United States Air Force, at the service of the CIA, crossed the Turkish-Soviet border near Yerevan while on a flight from Nicosia to Tehran. Two Russian pilots in MiG-17P Fresco fighters intercepted the plane 30km south of Yerevan, attacking it with cannon fire and forcing it to make an emergency landing on a half-built runway in Azerbaijan.[3, 4]

A month later, on 26 July 1958, a United States Air Force Boeing RB-47 Stratojet spy plane, the long-range reconnaissance adaptation of the namesake nuclear bomber, was intercepted by Soviet fighters over the Caspian Sea, 130 miles east-southeast of the city of Astara, Azerbaijan. The plane, which had departed from Iran, managed to evade the interceptors and returned undamaged to Tehran. A few days later, on 31 October 1958, another spy Boeing RB-47 Stratojet was attacked by Soviet fighters over the Black Sea, although its three crew members were unharmed and the plane returned in its entirety to its base, probably Aldana in Turkey.[5]

The Russian pilots' frenzy to shoot down anything entering Soviet airspace led them to attack even ostensibly, civilian planes that had incidentally crossed the border by mistake. On 4 August 1961, an Iranian Airways Douglas DC-4 cargo plane flying from Beirut to Tehran, was intercepted by unidentified fighter jets after accidentally crossing the Turkey-Armenia border. The aircraft sustained significant damage to the left wing and both of its outboard engines, forcing the crew to make an emergency, gear-retracted

The crew of the CL-44 of Transporte Aéreo Rioplatense shot down over Soviet Armenia on 18 July 1981. From left to right: Héctor Ismael Cordero Jaureguiberry (Airline Transport Pilot, commander), Hermete Mateo Boasso (Line Transport Pilot, 1st Officer), and José Raúl Burgueño (Technician/Flight Engineer). (La Semana)

landing in the Azerbaijan Soviet Republic on the southwestern coast of the Caspian Sea.[6]

In May 1963, a pair of MiG-17F Fresco fighters shot down an Aerocommander 560 of the Imperial Iranian Air Force over Azerbaijan, killing the entire crew, which included an American colonel in US Special Forces. Eight years later, in 1971, a USAF Lockheed C-130 Hercules was reported to have crashed in Iran while flying too close to the Soviet border. Although the identity of the aircraft or the extent of the damage suffered was never disclosed, there is no doubt that it was used for distant espionage tasks, since by then the Sun Valley model was already in service, the electronic warfare version of the Hercules, which could monitor Soviet radio broadcasts without entering their territory, simply by flying high over the very edge of the border.[7, 8]

On 20 November 1963, a MiG-19PM attacked with cannon fire, an Iranian Aero Commander L-26B civilian plane that had crossed the Soviet border. The circumstances of the episode or the place where it occurred have not been disclosed, it is only known that the plane ended up landing in Persian territory, severely damaged and that the subsequent investigation indicated that it was at the service of North American and Iranian intelligence. Another Aerocommander 560, this one from the Imperial Iranian Air Force, was shot down in August 1964 by a MiG-17 Fresco.[9]

Three years later, on 28 June 1967, a Russian fighter pilot forced an Iranian L-20 to land, although the circumstances and exact location of the incident have not been disclosed. That same year, an electronic espionage Boeing ERB-47H Stratojet operated by the USAF's 55th Strategic Reconnaissance Wing, taking off from Tehran for the purpose of sweeping the Soviet radio frequency spectrum with its sensors, was hit by a surface-to-air missile while it was still flying over Iran, very close to the border with the Soviet Union. The pilot tried to return to its base but ended up falling on the mountains north of the Iranian capital, resulting in the destruction of the aircraft and the total loss of the crew.[10]

On 11 September 1970, at 03:36 in the morning, a Soviet defence radar located in Sevastopol detected a suspicious plane flying at 260km per hour and 3,000 metres in the direction of the border and sent a red alert to all regiments in the area. When the target was 100km from the border, in a general southwest direction, a Sukhoi Su-15 from the 64th Fighter Aviation Regiment took off from Belbek (Russia) and went out to meet the aircraft. It was an old Douglas C-47 Skytrain freighter belonging to the Hellenic Air Force, whose pilot immediately agreed to the intercept signals given by the Russian pilot, by moving the wings of his plane. After the landing of both planes in Belbek, it turned out that the Greek freighter had been stolen from the Cania Kania base, in Crete, by Lieutenant M. Maniatakis, an officer who requested political asylum in the Soviet Union so as not to return to Greece, where a Military Junta had seized power.

On 21 October 1970, a twin-engined United States Air Force Beechcraft L-23/RU-8 Seminole accidentally veered off course, violated Soviet Union airspace and landed by mistake at the military airfield in Leninakan, Armenia. In addition to the pilot, the plane was carrying two American generals and a Turkish colonel. Realising his mistake, the pilot tried to take off again, but the head of the military unit, Commander Alexander Nikitovich Leonov, prevented him from doing so by passing a vehicle on the runway. The crew of the Seminole were arrested and released on 10 November 1970 after a rather lengthy (and humiliating) investigation.[11, 12]

These shoot-downs and unfortunate events with American-made aircraft did not intimidate the Iranians, much less the Turks, who as soon as they had high-speed aircraft, began to carry out provocative intrusions with the same flight patterns and with the same procedures that had come from the North Atlantic Treaty Organisation (NATO). On 7 September 1972, several North American F-100 Super Sabers of the Turkish Air Force made a low-altitude raid into Soviet airspace near Leninakan (Armenia). The radars quickly detected them, but when they flew together, they appeared on the screens as if they had been a single large plane, so only one Sukhoi Su-15 Flagon interceptor from the Fighter Aviation Regiment No. 166 based in Georgia was scrambled. When radar control realised the ruse, it was already too late and to make matters worse, the Su-15 could not fire because the raiders were flying too low. The four Turkish F-100s made a thunderous pass over an Armenian radar station and, after being taunted, returned to their home base with impunity.

The next visit of the Turks would come on 23 May 1975, when another F-100 Super Saber once again crossed the border limits of the Soviet Republic of Armenia. A Sukhoi Su-15 Flagon from the Kyurdamir base (Azerbaijan) was ordered to take off to intercept it, but once again the Turkish fighter entered an area protected by anti-aircraft missiles. One of the batteries fired a missile, but the homing failed and the F-100 managed to escape. The luck of the Turks would end on 24 August 1976, when radar operators detected in Turkish airspace an echo flying at high-speed towards the Armenian border. The signal was quickly identified as two Super Sabers flying in close formation. To intercept them, the Soviet defence ordered the take-off of at least three Su-15s from the Kyurdamir and Sandar bases, but once again the Super Sabers entered an area defended with missiles, so the Soviet fighters had to keep at a certain distance. In the end, one of the F-100s was shot down, but both the pilot and the wreckage of the plane went down on the Turkish side of the border. Turkey's graceful reactions to what was described as an 'unappealable Soviet aggression' did not wait.[13]

The suspicion of the Soviets before the incursions of photo-reconnaissance and electronic intelligence became such that they began to shoot down even the meteorological probe balloons that circumstantially entered their airspace carried by the wind, which can give an idea of the paranoia frenzy that had overwhelmed them in the Cold War. The NATO powers, for their part, did nothing to reduce that tension, as eager for information about the capabilities of their opponents (especially in terms of nuclear development, space technology and intercontinental ballistic missiles) they dedicated themselves to penetrating the territory 'enemy' as deep as possible.

On 21 July 1978, four Boeing CH-47C Chinook heavy helicopters of the Imperial Iranian Army penetrated between 15–20 kilometres into the airspace of Turkmenistan, being seen in the distance by a lone MiG-23M fighter whose pilot mistook them for Soviet units. Minutes later, the four Chinooks were intercepted by a second MiG-23M that attacked them firing R-60 (AA-8 Aphid) heat-seeking missiles, shooting down the first one and killing eight of its occupants. Running out of infrared missiles, the second pilot fired his GSh-23L 23mm high-velocity cannon at another Chinook, forcing it to land near the town of Gjaurs. All four crew members survived but were captured by Soviet border guards. The two remaining Chinooks escaped into Iranian territory.[14]

At 14:57 (Moscow time) on 23 December 1979, a small Cessna 185 Skywagon reconnaissance aircraft entered Soviet airspace from Iran 175km (108 nautical miles) from Maryy, Turkmen Soviet Republic. The plane, which was flying at an altitude of 3,000 metres, was detected by air defence radar just three minutes before it crossed the border, for which a Sukhoi Su-15 of the 156 Fighter Aviation

Regiment was dispatched to intercept it, stationed at the Maryy-2 airbase. The Soviet pilot was guided to the interception point by the command and control centre, but upon arrival he found nothing, so he kept flying in circles and after a while, returned to his base. By that time, three more Su-15s and one MiG-23M from nearby bases were already on alert, but none were taken off as the target had simply disappeared. However, it turned out that the target was there and that the mission had been successfully accomplished by the first interceptor; when the Iranian Air Force pilot saw the Su-15 appear overhead, he immediately aborted his spy mission, rapidly lost altitude and landed on a highway 195km from Maryy, where he was captured by border guards before whom he claimed a navigation error. His plane, small and camouflaged, simply could not be seen from the air by the fighter pilot.

However, the most notable demolition that occurred on the southern border of the Soviet Union and the one that would be most remembered in the classrooms of its military academies, was the one carried out on 28 November 1973 by the pilot Gennadii N. Eliseev, of the Regiment of Fighter Aviation 982, who intercepted with his MiG-21SM Fishbed, an Imperial Iranian Air Force RF-4E Phantom II photo-reconnaissance aircraft over Mugavská, Azerbaijan. After two failed attempts to fire his infrared-seeking AA-2 Atoll missiles and in the midst of a frantic chase over the Azeri mountains and deserts, Eliseev realised that the Phantom would escape him behind the Iranian border, so he decided to take him down at any cost, even at the cost of his own life. Not caring about the consequences from him, Elissev rammed his MiG into the Phantom, but in doing so smashed his own plane, which crashed out of control into the ground, killing him instantly. Upon receiving the impact of the MiG, the Phantom also destabilised, hitting the ground, but its crew managed to eject in time.

The Phantom's pilot, Major Shokouhnia, was from the Imperial Iranian Air Force, while its electronic operator, Colonel John Saunders, was a United States Air Force officer. When questioned after their rescue, they claimed to have been lost during a training flight, although it was clear that they were carrying out an intelligence mission inside Soviet territory with a specially prepared plane. In fact, it was one of the secret flights of Operation Dark Gene, specifically designed to detect anti-aircraft missile sites near the Soviet border. The two crew members of the Phantom were released days later (formally in exchange for the image cartridge from a Soviet reconnaissance satellite that had accidentally gone down in Iran), so that their testimony could serve as endorsement of the Russian determination to prevent intrusions into their airspace. Gennadii Eliseev received the posthumous title of Hero of the Soviet Union and his death was taken as an example of courage and sacrifice to be emulated by all pilots of all air defence squadrons. The crew of the Phantom were also decorated by the government of the Shah of Iran, although Major Shokouhnia ended up being executed in 1980 as part of the purges ordered by the government of the Islamic Revolution.[15, 16]

Starting in 1980 and as the Cold War heated up, provocation flights near the Turkish-Soviet border became more frequent, especially since the psychological harassment operations devised by the United States Department of Defense to get on the nerves of the Russians. Symmetrically, the member countries of NATO were armed to the teeth, forcing the Russians to make an equivalent expense in defence matters, which ultimately undermined the communist economy, which did not have the wealth creation dynamic of capitalism. Turkey being a member of NATO, its Air Force (Turk Hava Kuvvetleri) was equipped with the best and most modern in the Western arsenal.[17]

By 1981, the Turkish Air Force had an enviable American-built fleet, including six squadrons of McDonnell-Douglas F-4E and RF-4E Phantoms based at Eskisehir and Erhac bases, five squadrons of Lockheed F-104G/TF-104G Starfighter based at Murted, Bandirma, Merzifon and Balikeshir, two squadrons of North American F-100C/D/F Super Saber at Diyarbakir, four squadrons of Northrop F-5A/B and RF-5A Tiger based at Bandirma Diyarbakir, Konya and Merzifon. United States military aid to Turkey had been interrupted in 1975 as a result of the Turkish invasion of the island of Cyprus, during which time Washington was unable to maintain the 26 bases it had deployed on its territory (most of them radar stations) for the survey intelligence data on the other side of the Soviet border), but they recovered them in 1978, months before the Islamic Revolution broke out in Iran.[18]

By far, the most important of those US-Turkish bases was Pirinçlik, near the town of Diyarbakir, for the purpose of providing NATO electronic surveillance over the airspace of the Soviet Union, the Caucasus and the Middle East. To this end, it had, among other systems, two automated radars that provided continuous intelligence information, observed the deep airspace inside the border and could even produce early warnings before the launch of nuclear-headed missiles. An AN/FPS-17 detection radar and an AN/FPS-79 mechanical tracking radar were mounted at Pirinçlik, both operated in the 432 MegaHertz ultra-high frequency band. The

The electronic intelligence station at Pirinçlik, near Diyarbakir, in Turkey, in 1981. It was from there that the 7022nd Air Base Squadron of the 39th Tactical Group US Air Force, monitored all aerial movements over the southern Soviet Union. (Guido Ghiretti)

Antenna of the powerful AN/FPS-17 over-the-horizon radar installed near Diyarbakir, capable of tracking launches of the Soviet missiles from the Kapustin Yar cosmodrome. (Guido Ghiretti)

FPS-17s were fixed and their antennas were oriented towards the Soviet Union, while the FPS-79s had a 10 metre diameter antenna and a variable focus system that allowed them to detect distant targets, with a maximum effective range of 4,300km. These radars gave NATO the advantage of simultaneously tracking multiple targets in real time, being the only Western ground station capable of tracking orbital re-entries of Soviet spacecraft, ballistic missiles or space debris. In addition, Pirinçlik's radar was the only one in the eastern hemisphere with a deep-space sensor capable of operating 24 hours a day, every day of the year. The base was managed by the 7022 Air Base Squadron of the 39 Tactic Group of the United States Air Force.[19, 20, 21, 22, 23]

The NATO radar stations installed in Turkey were particularly attentive to everything that moved towards, over or through the northern border of the country (which marked the south of the Soviet Union), but from 22 September 1980, the start date of the Iran-Iraq War, were also very alert to what was happening on the eastern border (border with Iran) and on the southern border (border with Iraq). Observing both combatants in an air war context was very instructive for NATO considering that the Iraqi air forces were mainly equipped with Soviet equipment, thus following Soviet tactics and flight patterns. On the other hand, the Iranians followed American tactics since all their pilots had been trained in the United States and operated in American planes. Therefore, observing how they fought each other represented an excellent laboratory for experimentation for Western analysts, since it was reasonable to assume that the yields, casualties and tricks used or suffered by, each side represented, on a scale, what could be the scenario of a Third World War fought with conventional weapons – not atomic.

The surveillance of the NATO stations on the Turkish border with Iran and Iraq increased from 4 April 1981, when the Iranian Air Force launched one of its most daring missions against an Iraqi airbase, the airfield complex called H-3, located deep in the western end of Iraq, specifically in the town of Al-Waleed, near Turkey. At that point in the rear, the Iraqis had sheltered their entire fleet of bombers, in the certainty that they would never be hit by the Persians, who to travel there would have to fly over all of Iraq and its multiple anti-aircraft defences. However, Iranian Air Force strategists thought otherwise and in fact, had been contemplating an attack on the H-3 complex since the first day of the war. The main problem was that to carry out such a long-distance operation, the raiders had to operate from Turkey.[24]

For this operation, 10 F-4 Phantom II fighter-bombers from the 31st and 32nd Tactical Fighter Wing, two F-14A Tomcats, a C-130H Khofaash for communications and intelligence, a Boeing 747 for air control and tanker and two Boeing 707-J29C tankers. The plan was simple but daring: using the confusion created by a diversionary strike against targets in the Kirkuk region, a formation of eight F-4s was to penetrate deep into Iraq, rendezvous with the two Boeing 707 tankers, and surprise attack the H-3 complex from the north from where the Iraqis would not expect any attack.

To achieve this, several hours before the attack, the two Boeing 707 tankers took off from Istanbul International Airport, in Turkey and secretly diverted from the civil airway through which they were to fly to Tehran. In total radio silence, they descended over southern Turkey, entering Syrian eastern airspace and rejoined the Phantom formation over the western Iraqi desert. What followed was an extraordinarily complicated aerial refuelling operation with each of the fighter-bombers refuelling four times in formation just 100 metres above the desert to stay below the horizon of Iraqi radars. The attack took the H-3 complex completely by surprise, causing the total destruction of three Antonov An-12BP transports, one Tu-16 bomber, four MiG-21 fighters, five Su-20/-22 fighters, eight MiG-23, two Mirage F-1EQ and four Mil Mi-8 helicopters and severely damaging 11 other aircraft. During the return, in-flight refuelling occurred mostly over Syrian airspace. NATO analysts were puzzled not only by the audacity of the Iranian attack on the Iraqi rear, but also because half of its flight time had been spent over Turkish and Syrian airspace.[25]

The attack on the H-3 complex also stunned Soviet analysts, who watched the Iran-Iraq War with the same interest and purpose as their Western counterparts. It was likely that the Iraqis would try to strike back with a surprise attack on Iran from the northwest, for which they would have to enter Turkish airspace. For this reason and due to the continued fear of receiving a surprise attack by NATO forces based in Turkey, from 4 April 1981, the Soviet defence increased surveillance on its southern border, particularly in the

Electronic surveillance station of the Royal Air Force at Ayios Nicolaos, on Cyprus, as seen in 1981. Already at the time, this station was capable of monitoring the mass of aerial movements in the Mediterranean and the Middle East – and thus the passages of the Canadair CL-44 of TAR were unlikely to remain undetected by the British intelligence. (Julian Nitzsche)

Electronic warfare station of the Royal Air Force at Troodos, on Cyprus, in 1981. Along with Ayios Nicolaos, its radars and sensors were integrated into the Echelon intelligence network: as a result, nothing moved in the skies above the eastern Mediterranean without being detected. (Roy Lambeth)

Transcaucasia military district, which included the Soviet Republics of Georgia, Armenia and Azerbaijan.

Thus, when on the night of 17 July 1981, the Canadair CL-44 freighter of TAR departed from its airway to 'cut the road' to Tehran, flying in a straight line over the Ararat mountains, its echo radar triggered the alert of the entire Soviet Air Defence. Minutes later, when the bright spot shown on the screens entered Armenian airspace, phones began to ring frantically in the office of Colonel Grechko, Head of the Aviation Forces of the Transcaucasian Military District, based in Tbilisi, Georgia, to whom the overflight of Soviet territory by 'a spy plane' was reported. Before the Tbilisi control centre could order the interceptors to launch, the intruder on radar reached the Iranian border.[26]

Grechko ordered to document the incident and reported it to Moscow. The same was done by the operational guard of the Tbilisi interception control centre, through the Anti-aircraft Defence Radiotechnical Command. Immediately, the Ministry of Defence of the Soviet Union ordered the dispatch of a commission of technicians and analysts to investigate the behaviour adopted by the intruder aircraft and at the same time, the reaction of the entire interception system when faced with the event. For Colonel Grechko, this meant not only a comprehensive audit of the image and audio records of the radar network, but a performance review of all officers and technicians involved in the chain of command. Knowing that he would be thoroughly investigated and anticipating that the commission would arrive in Tbilisi in a matter of hours, not days, he put all the airbases in his jurisdiction on alert, especially those of Kyurdamir and Nasosnaya (Azerbaijan), Vaziani and Marneuli (Georgia). Radar operators were asked to sharpen their senses, in case the strange echo appeared on their screens again. To show diligence in front of the investigative commission, Grechko ordered to set up defensive patrols with flying fighters along the entire southern border of the Transcaucasian Military District, which had to rotate with their relief guards in 24 hour shifts.[27]

So, by the night of 17 July 1981, the entire Soviet Air Defence of the Transcaucasian Military District was already on guard and ready to intercept the cargo plane that they suspected would try to cut the path again over Azerbaijan or Armenia on its way back from Iran to Turkey. What radar operators and pilots did not know was that the KGB already had the electronic decoy set up that would take the plane directly into its jaws.

8

COVERT SHOOTING DOWN IN ARMENIA

The Mossad, the Israeli intelligence service, planned for Friday 17 July 1981, the third secret flight that the Canadair CL-44 registration LV-JTN of Transporte Aéreo Rioplantese, was to carry out from Tel Aviv to Iran, within the framework of Operation Seashell. The cargo consisted mainly of cannon tubes, tank spare parts, spare parts for combat aircraft, and 105mm artillery shells. According to the false documentation made for the flight, the plane would fly empty, although in reality it was fully loaded. The crew was made up of Commander Héctor Cordero Jaureguiberry, co-pilot Hermete Mateo Boasso and mechanic José Raúl Burgueño, who would be accompanied, as always, by Stuart McCafferty, in charge of the real and forged documents. As in the previous cases, the freighter would not be announced to air traffic services with its Argentine

Yuri Vladimirovich Andropov, director of the powerful KGB from 1967 until 1982. Under his command, the Soviet intelligence organised the interception operation of the Argentine aircraft involved in the secret shipments of arms from Israel to Iran. (TASS)

Vladimir Aleksandrovich Kryuchkov, Director of Foreign Intelligence Department of the KGB between 1974 and 1988, and responsible for the decoy operation that was to expose the arms trafficking of Operation Seashell. (TASS)

General Semyon Kuzmich Tsvigun, Deputy Director of the KGB at the time of planning of the interception of the CL-44 of TAR. (TASS)

General Marius Aramovich Yuzbahyan, head of the KGB in the Soviet Armenia at the time of the planning of the interception of the Argentine CL-44. (TASS)

registration, but with the flight codes granted by Israel and Iran to the company Afro Continental Airways for the outbound (KY223) and return legs. (YR224). These codes, of course, were fake. [1]

The third flight from Tel Aviv to Iran was direct, without a stopover at Larnaca or any other airport. It is highly possible that the plane followed exactly the same airways, flying over Cyprus but not landing, thus distancing its presence on the island. Despite this and other safeguards, the Israeli and Iranian intelligence services could not prevent the large movements of air cargo to Tehran from being detected by their Soviet counterpart, the Committee for State Security (Komitet Gosudárstvennoy Bezopásnosti), whose title in Russian language the acronym KGB was formed.[2]

By June 1981, the KGB was already clear about the whole picture, to such an extent that they allowed themselves to warn the Israeli secret service they were aware of their actions. In the words of Ari Ben-Menashe, one of the Israeli brains behind Operation Seashell,

> Toward the end of June [1981] we heard from the KGB. The intelligence and security service of the Soviet Union, through its representative in Israel, presented a formal letter of request to the head of the office of the Director of Military Intelligence [General Yehoshua Sagi], coming from the Directorate of Foreign Affairs of the KGB. The letter requested explanations from Israel about flights originating in Tel Aviv that flew close to the Turkish-Soviet border and landed in Tehran. The head of Sagi's office passed the letter to me and I presented it to the Israel Defence Forces/Military Industries-Mossad working committee for Israel-Iran relations. I considered that an explanation could be given to the Soviets. But Israeli arrogance came into play. The prevailing view, without consulting the Prime Minister's [Menashe Begin] office, was to respond to the letter by arguing that the Israeli government did not discuss its foreign and security policies. It was an abrupt and stupid response. Signed by the IDF/MI head of Foreign Affairs, it was handed over to the Soviet representative in Israel in the first week of July. [3]

The haughty response from the Jews only served to provoke the Russians and this was perhaps the biggest mistake that Israeli intelligence could make, as bent as it was on the secrecy of Operation Seashell. In a bipolar world in which the the Soviet Union ranked as a superpower, the KGB could not be snubbed without paying the consequences. Thus, under the supervision of Vladimir Kryuchkov (head of the First Directorate of the KGB) and with the authorisation of General Semyon Kuzmich Tsvigun (vice president of the KGB), the Soviet secret service began to organise the intelligence operation which would give a lesson to the Mossad.

The chosen format was quite simple and consisted of causing a diversion into Soviet airspace of some of the civilian aircraft involved in Operation Seashell, by emitting false radio signals that confused the pilots or navigation systems. Once the plane had crossed the border, all that had to be done was intercept it according to international air navigation rules and force it to land at some airport inside the border. Once on the ground, it would be easy to expose the whole scheme of Israel's clandestine arms sales to Iran.

An inside view at the radio interference station of Popovka, near Leningrad, in the USSR. Its dimensions and equipment were similar to those of the Gavar station in Soviet Armenia. (Rimantas Pielkys)

The Tbilisi command and control centre, in the Soviet Republic of Georgia, as of 1981. Each post with its own screen represented one of the major early warning/surveillance radar stations of the Transcaucasian Military District. Visible on the wall at the top of the photograph, is a general map of the entire region, including Armenia, Azerbaijan, Turkey and northern Iran. The entire system was managed with help of the Vozdukh-1M integrated air defence system, which communicated with Su-15 interceptors with help of the Lazur data-link and Bumerang-1 computer system. (V-PVO)

In addition, the operation would bring enormous political gain to the Soviet Union since the American origin of the weapons could not be hidden, thus discrediting the entire US embargo and the very bellicose President Reagan. The coup would also affect Iran, whose Islamic Revolution was by definition religious and therefore anti-communist, directly threatening Soviet interests throughout Asia and the Far East, but especially in Afghanistan, where Russian soldiers were already facing the religious fanaticism of the early Taliban rebels. Pulling back the curtain on Operation Seashell could also be useful for Moscow's diplomatic and trade relations with the Baghdad government, especially since the Iraqi armed forces were fighting their war against Iran with Soviet-made weapons.

Broadcasting false radio navigation signals as a decoy to lure aircraft into one's own territory was part of the electronic warfare that Soviet intelligence services continually played against their NATO counterparts. One of its main manifestations was jamming, deliberate radio interference, generated to reflect or 'screen' electromagnetic signals in order to deprive the intended target of the use of electronic devices, equipment or systems, for example by erasing or obscuring the signals that an aircraft was trying to receive. It was accomplished by using multiple carrier antennas tuned to the victim's frequency or amplitude modulating random noise, driving simulated traffic on the target frequency, generating a continuous wave (keyed or steady) or generating multiple audio tones in rapid sequence (in electronic warfare jargon called bagpipes due to its characteristic sound). [4, 5, 6, 7, 8, 9, 10]

To the delight of the KGB, into the Armenian territory had been built one of the most powerful interference stations in the entire Soviet Union, specifically the Gavar station, located at coordinates

Antennas for radio interference (or 'jamming') of the standard type as used by the Soviet intelligence services. Those installed at Gavar would have been the same size. (Rimantas Pleykis)

40° 25' 32.68" North Latitude – 45° 12' 16.15" East Longitude. Its antenna, with 1,000 kilowatts of power, was one of the tallest constructions in the Soviet Union (it stood 259.40 metres above the ground) and could transmit in a frequency range ranging from 100 to 17,600 Kilohertz. To give an idea of its capacity, it is enough to indicate that its shielding and radio interference could reach Poland.[11, 12]

The final details of the operation that would allow one of the civilian freighters carrying weapons to Iran to be 'hunted down' were closed with Colonel Marius Aramovich Yuzbahyan, head of the Armenian KGB section and General Pyotr I. Ivashutin, head of the Central Department of Intelligence of the Soviet Armed Forces or GRU (acronym of Glávnoye Razvédyvatelnoye Upravlenie). Everything indicates that the mechanism used was to calibrate one of the antennas of the Gavar Armenian station so that it would transmit exactly on the 115.2 Megahertz frequency corresponding to the omnidirectional radio beacon located in the Turkish town of Van. In parallel, the emission of a second false signal would have been programmed from the 311.7 metre high communication tower located in the city of Yerevan (40° 10' 16.7" North Latitude, 44° 32' 11.49" Longitude East), to pretend to be the *Very High Frecuency Omni-directional Range* (VOR) station of the Turkish city of Erzurum, which transmitted on the frequency of 112.4 Megahertz.

When these two decoys were turned on simultaneously, any plane coming from Iran could deviate grossly from its route, enter Soviet space and be at the mercy of interceptor fighters. The false signals could not remain permanently active, at the risk of confusing all commercial air traffic flying between Iran and Turkey. For this reason, precise radar tracking of the chosen target was necessary, whose take-off had to be previously reported by KGB agents stationed at the Larnaka, Ankara or Tehran airports. At a certain moment, the electronic measures would be activated until the desired purpose was achieved.[13]

Once the duped plane entered Soviet airspace, the interception could be directed by any fighter from any air defence regiment. The location and time of activation of the electronic decoys would not be reported to the air bases, most likely to guarantee the secrecy of the operation and incidentally, to check in real conditions what the response speed and professional performance of the pilots could be. Given the geographical location of the Gavar and Yerevan radio stations, everything indicated that the Tbilisi radar control centre would assign the interception to planes from the 982 Fighter Aviation Regiment based at the Vaziani Air Base, an exclusively military airfield located in the Georgian Soviet Republic. The unit was attached to the 283rd Fighter Aviation Division of the 34th Air Army and was equipped with MiG-23MLA/MLD fighters.[14, 15]

The intercepted civil plane had to be forced to land at the Zvartnots International Airport, then the main one in Armenia, located about 10km west of Yerevan, simply because it was the closest to the border. This airport had been inaugurated in 1961 and had a formidable, paved runway 3,849 metres long with orientation 09/27, which certainly had the capacity to receive large aircraft.[16, 17]

Although they had no chance of knowing it, the crew of the Canadair CL-44 of TAR were about to be led into a trap that, in principle, would only cause them a few hours of delay at the Zvartnots Airport in Yerevan. No one, not even the Russians themselves, knew when or where their plane (or any other plane in the service of Operation Seashell) would take the electronic bait and cross the Soviet border. What the KGB planners were completely certain of was that the plane and its crew would be released almost immediately, since the objective of the operation was not to interdict a plane, much less to apprehend its occupants, but to expose clandestine arms transfer from Israel to Iran. The crew members were just pawns on the huge chessboard where the master move of intelligence was about to unfold – nothing more. Unfortunately, the entire planned KGB interception would end up going horribly wrong.

On 18 July 1981, at the precise moment when the Canadair CL-44 of TAR took off empty from Tehran's Mehrabad airport, to begin its return to Tel Aviv in ballast, a KGB agent stationed outside the airport reported its departure to the Soviet embassy in Tehran by telephone, probably with a simple 'wrong number' call. From the embassy, through an encrypted system, the air defence control centre in Tbilisi, Georgia was notified. Minutes later, the Soviet Union's radars already had on their screens a slowly rising echo flying northwest, whose communications in English with the Tehran Area Control Centre (ACC) could be heard perfectly on the radio frequency. The aircraft departed to the northwest along the airway that marked the 289° radial of the Tehran VOR station until it reached the Zanján aerodrome, 137 nautical miles away from the starting point. Following the instrumental navigation chart, Commander Cordero mounted the 286° radial of the Zanján VOR heading towards the Uromiyeh airport, located on the western shore of the homonymous lake, 185 nautical miles away.

At 11:48 a.m. from Tehran, the Argentine plane contacted the Ankara ACC, in Turkey, on the radio frequency of 129.45 Megahertz, reporting that it had already passed the BONAM position, the point of

The KV-5 high power transmitters installed at the Vilnius communications-jamming station, in Soviet Lithuania. The equipment was of the same type as that installed at the Gavar station. (Rimantas Pleikys)

notification located right on the Iran-Turkey border, practically in the middle of the airway linking Uromiyeh airport to Turkey's Van airport. A minute later, Canadair reported that it planned to block the Van airport VOR at 10:26 Ankara time and then head to the Tatvan VOR, from there to the Turkish Erzurum airport VOR, then Gemerek airport and then the Turkish airport VOR. The Ankara control centre replied that the plane should block Van and then fly on the W27 airway directly to Erzurum, to then block the VOR of Turkey's Sivas airport.[18 19]

At the moment they heard that the communications pass from Iranian to Turkish air traffic control was taking place (which meant that the pilots of the Argentine plane would be busy changing the tuning of the plane's main radio), the stations Yerevan and Gavar Armenians activated their electronic radio jamming mechanisms. From then on, a radio signal calibrated on the same frequency as the VOR of the Turkish Van airport began to emit from Armenian territory with much higher power, at the same time as the disturbance of the link to and from the plane that was communicating with Ankara began. The electronic web had been activated and it was only to be hoped that the Canadair would be caught in it like a fly.

The Argentine crew took the bait. At a certain point, Soviet (and Turkish) radars noticed that the plane unexpectedly turned north, heading directly for the tripoint, the place where the borders of Turkey, Iran and the Soviet Union meet, at 39° 38' North Latitude – 44° 49' East Longitude. The detour was so rude, so pronounced, that it was also detected by the air traffic radar at the Tabriz airport (38° 7' 55' North Latitude – 46° 14' 25' West Longitude), where the second Tactical Air Base was located of the Iranian Air Force, which at the time was overflowing with Northrop F-5 Tiger fighters. It is extremely likely that, upon noticing the diversion, the Tabriz control tried to contact the Argentine plane, but it is also very likely that the calls were not even heard on board, as Canadair was in communication with the centre of control of Ankara and, moreover, already subject to radio disturbances generated from Gavar. Consequently, the Argentine freighter continued to fly north, passing over the Tabriz control area without even knowing where it was flying.

At 10:30 a.m. local Turkey time, the Ankara ACC contacted Canadair asking if it had already blocked the Van airport position, as according to their estimates this had already occurred. The response from the freighter was that they still had not. Immediately afterwards, from the Argentine plane, Commander Cordero (or co-pilot Boasso) asked ground control if the Van VOR-DME radio aid station was in service. It was evident that Cordero suspected something, as through the radio compass he must have noticed that his plane was flying to the north, when in fact he should be flying to the west. Ankara asked to repeat the question and did so a total of seven times without getting an answer, probably because the radio shielding produced by the Soviets was working perfectly. Everything suggests that, upon hearing this communication, the Russian electronic warfare officers stopped issuing the decoy signal on the Van VOR frequency, changing it to the Turkish Erzurum airport VOR frequency, to further confuse their deceived target.

The Argentine crew should have seen the VOR-DME system indicator signal go crazy, now showing Van airport in its true position, which had fallen behind the aircraft. Thus, at 10:43 a.m. (local Turkish time) the CL-44 replied to Ankara control that it had checked the Van position at flight level 220 (22,000 feet). By this time, the sound of the communication was already weak in Ankara, as if the Canadair was getting further and further away from Turkey instead of getting closer – which indeed was happening. In the last seconds of audible communication, the aircraft replied that it estimated to block the Erzurum VOR beacon at 10:58 hours. Aware of the weakness of the radio signal, the Ankara air traffic controller instructed the aircraft to communicate with Erzurum on the frequency of 127.3 Megahertz if it could hear but by then, the radio link was extremely weak. Ankara called three times at 10:44 a.m. (local) without receiving any response. The controller's last attempt occurred at 10:54 a.m. but contact with the Argentine aircraft had been completely lost.

As soon as the Tbilisi air defence control centre warned that the deceived plane's entry into Soviet airspace was inevitable, it ordered four planes from the 982 Fighter Aviation Regiment to take off from the Vaziani Air Base, so that they could fly out to meet them. – it was 2:30 p.m. Tbilisi time. According to the KGB plan, the fighters were to catch up with the freighter, intercept it in accordance with international rules and bring it to land at Zvartnots airport, near the city of Yerevan. The operation would be led from the Tbilisi control centre by Colonel Grechko, commander of the Soviet Air Force (VVS) in the Transcaucasus Military District and by Colonel Ashot Bagdasarian, head of the Soviet Air Defence (PVO) of the same district., who reported to all operators of the complex Vozdukh-1M intercept guidance system. As it could not be otherwise, the ongoing operation was known to Colonel General Oleg Fyodorovich

An aerial view of the CL-44 LV-JTN. The letters of the registration, logo and the title of the TAR are all clearly visible – even from a position and distance from which the aircraft must have been seen by all the Soviet pilots that tried to intercept it, including Captain Valentin Kulyapin. (Héctor Biondini)

Koulishev, Commander of the entire Transcaucasia Military District.[20, 21, 22, 23]

In accordance with international regulations, the aircraft in charge of the interception had to approach the target from behind ('from the stern'), move forward to a position that allowed it to be clearly seen from the cockpit of the intercepted aircraft (preferably appearing from the left) and bank sharply to get the attention of the other pilot. The intercepted pilot was expected to respond to the warning by moving the wings of his own aircraft at the same time and follow the interceptor towards the indicated course, in this case the Yerevan airport. Whatever the number of fighters that reached the target, only one had to go ahead to comply with the interception procedure, the rest had to remain formed at a safe distance of at least 500 feet (about 150 metres) to monitor the behaviour of the intercepted aircraft and identify it by registering its licence plate, flag, colours and eventually, trademarks. In addition to following the interceptor fighter, the intercepted aircraft had the obligation to contact it by radio on the 121.5 Megahertz frequency and at the same time, contact air traffic services to inform them of its identity, the purpose of the flight and the position at the time of the intercept.[24]

The entire intercept procedure involved the intercepting aircraft matching the intercepted in speed, forming wing-to-wing to the left and then slowly moving forward to be seen from the cockpit by the other pilot. It was precisely with this manoeuvre, apparently so simple, that the four Sukhoi Su-15TM fighters dispatched from Vaziani began to have problems as soon as they encountered the Transporte Aéreo Rioplatense Canadair, which entered Soviet airspace at 2:37 p.m. (Moscow summer time) practically over the town of Nakhchivan, in the Azerbaijan Soviet Republic. It appeared that the Argentine plane was flying at its cruising rate of 621 kilometres per hour, an astonishingly slow speed for a Su-15 fighter, whose cruising rate was 1,700 kilometres per hour.[25]

The Soviet fighters could regulate their speed by reducing the power of their two powerful Tumansky R-13-300 turbines and even applying air brakes, but the Canadair was flying at an altitude of 22,000 feet (6,700 metres), where the atmosphere is much thinner than at sea level, so the coefficient lift on the wings of fighters was drastically reduced. The wings of the Su-15, whose profile had been designed to achieve sustained supersonic flight, were calculated to begin to sustain at 370 kilometres per hour. But that number corresponded to lift at sea level. As the altitude increased, the stall speed decreased because the atmosphere was less dense. Thus, at the level and speed at which the Argentine plane was flying, the interception procedure became torture, as when trying to equalise the speed of the CL-44, the Su-15s were dangerously close to stalling.[26]

For the Tbilisi control centre, the situation began to spiral out of control as the four fighters were getting into trouble over Azerbaijan. All the theoretical training and all the practical exercises of the operators of the Vozdukh-1M system had been developed

A Sukhoi Su-15 interceptor of the V-PVO, seen airborne and armed with two R-98 missiles under its wings. This is how all the jets that failed to effect an intercept of the LV-JTN, must have looked when seen from the cockpit of the Argentine transport. (Guido Chiretti collection)

contemplating war scenarios in which the interceptor fighters climbed at supersonic speed to their target, enslaving it on their Taifun radar at variable distances of between 35 and 70 kilometres depending on whether it was an enemy fighter or bomber and then they fired R-98 missiles to bring it down. Slow-target interception exercises had been virtually non-existent as the chances of a stealth-attack nuclear bomber entering Soviet territory at low-speed were nil. It was exceedingly difficult to imagine that the slow target was also a civil aircraft flying at high altitude, since in Soviet airspace, as well as in Turkish and Iranian airspace, flying outside airways was prohibited.

To further complicate matters, it turned out that, after making several passes to the CL-44, the four Soviet pilots began to report fuel shortages in their respective planes. This information was also visible by telemetry at the Tbilisi command posts, as the Vozdukh-1M system made it possible to represent on the ground, the flight parameters and reserves of the aircraft it was guiding. The only alternative to continue with the interception was to summon other fighters to take over from Vaziani's four planes. At 1:30 p.m. (Georgia local time), when the fuel level of the four interceptors had reached half, Colonel Ashot Bagdasarian ordered two more fighters to take off from Marneuli Air Base.

The Taifun radar of the Su-15, as seen in 'open' condition, with radome of the jet removed for maintenance purposes. The system enabled target detection and tracking, and deployment of R-98 semi-active radar homing air-to-air missiles (NATO reporting name 'AA-3 Anab'). (V-PVO)

A view at one of two Kaliningrad R-98 missiles installed on a hardpoint under the left wing of a Su-15TM interceptor. Usually, each jet would carry one missile with a semi-active radar homing seeker head and one with infrared homing seeker head. The missile was armed with a hefty, 40kg warhead, could reach the speed of Mach 2.5, and had a maximum effective range of 19km (infrared homing version) or 24km (semi-active radar homing version). (V-PVO)

The duo was led by Captain Valentin Kulyapin, who used the call-sign 733 so that his name and rank could not be identified in communications with the control and command post, a routine measure in the Soviet Air Defence to give as little information as possible to Americans, Turks, or Iranians who might be listening on the frequency.

As soon as the pair of interceptors took off from Marneuli, Kulyapin made radio contact with the Tbilisi interception centre so that they could proceed to guide him towards the target that was being tracked by the Vozdukh-1M system. Hearing the tone of the communications between Tifis and Vaziani's four planes on the radio, the young pilot understood that something serious was happening at the border. Adrenaline began to flow through his veins and it was clear that he was not in the presence of an exercise but a real hostile situation, probably the interception of a spy plane or a NATO bomber. Thus, while he accelerated up to the flight level that had been indicated, Kulyapin strained his ears to get all the information possible, since he was being guided towards an 'active' target. Cautious listening paid off, as at one point he heard one of Vaziani's pilots indicate that the target outwardly resembled an

Hermete Mateo Boasso (right) seated in co-pilot's position of an CL-44 of the TAR. (Héctor Biondini)

José Raúl Burgeno in front of the instrument console of the Flight Engineer station of the CL-44 with registration LV-JTN. (Héctor Biondini)

Ilyushin IL-18 four-engine plane and that it was 'galloping past' and then making a turn.[27, 28, 29]

Kulyapin had no trouble figuring out the problem that was preventing the interception by Vaziani's fighters. It was clear that there was a significant speed difference between the jets and the target, so he had to prepare for low-speed flight if he wanted to complete the mission they had been unable to accomplish. However, to do this he had to get there fast, otherwise the prey could slip away to the other side of the border. Therefore, upon reaching 13,000 metres of altitude, he accelerated his plane to beyond the speed of sound, leaving his partner behind to gain the full attention of the Tbilisi command post. By the time he emerged from supersonic and was over his assigned area, he was informed by Tbilisi control that the target was directly below and slightly behind him, flying at almost half speed and 8,000 metres altitude. Kulyapin reduced power and gently dived his fighter.

Although the control centre did not order him to do so, he turned on the search radar to locate the intruder plane and as soon as he could see its silhouette in the distance, he turned it off and reported to the ground that he had the target in sight. There was tension and anxiety in the communications from Tbilisi, as minutes after the failed interception of Vaziani's fighters, the Canadair had re-entered Turkish airspace, but immediately afterwards, it had returned to fly over Soviet territory. The freighter was not zigzagging – at that moment it was going in a straight line, practically skirting the border. In actuality, down below, the border line was changing according to geographical features, specifically the course of the Aras river, which marked the political limit between Iran and Turkey (on one side), Azerbaijan and Armenia (on the other). Since the geographic map was perfectly delimited on the radar screens, the operators of the Vozdukh-1M system were fearful of continuing to guide the Russian pilot every time his target left Soviet jurisdiction or got too close to the foreign jurisdiction.

At a certain point, Kulyapin finally managed to see his target and presciently gradually reduced his speed to match that of the 'target'. As he did so, he raised the nose of his plane higher and higher, until it kept at an angle of 10 degrees above the horizon line, thus allowing the small wings of the Su-15TM to 'sweep' more air and continue to support despite the low density of the atmosphere. At first, when he was some distance away, the young Russian pilot identified the Canadair as 'a four-engine military transport with no nationality markings'. As he approached from the left, he could not see the title TAR, which had been erased on that very side at the Batch-Air workshop in Miami. If he could perfectly see the TAR logo painted on the drift, he figured something: 'like the sign of yin and yang'. He was also able to see the freighter's registration and even report it, although he did not know which country the LV-JTN registration might belong to.[30]

As soon as the Tbilisi command and control centre detected by radar that Pilot 733's aircraft had become close enough to the freighter (and that it had not overshot it like its predecessors), it ordered the plane to start the intercept procedure, 'forcing' the intruder aircraft to land at Zvartnots International Airport. Kulyapin knew full well that this meant moving ahead of the target to the left so as to be seen from his cockpit, then flapping his wings until the other plane did the same, at which point he was to guide it to the Yerevan airport. However, flapping his wings at that speed would mean losing the lift he was having such difficultly to maintain, automatically causing a spin. On the other hand, he interpreted that moving forward would mean 'turning his back' on an aircraft that, in his indoctrinated mind, he had already classified as hostile. For both reasons, Kulyapin tried to maintain his lateral position, inform Tbilisi of the movements of the plane that he considered 'intercepted' and wait for instructions, since the entire logic of the Soviet defence system was based on the fact that the pilots were not autonomous, but the executing arm from the command centre on the ground.

Commander Cordero did not see Kulyapin's Su-15TM in its approach phase and it is highly probable that he did not see it until sometime after it formed up. He must have been discussing with co-pilot Boasso the real position of the Canadair, checking charts with his head down or focusing on the cockpit dashboard to select VOR-DME stations that would let him know exactly where he was. Realising that he had a Soviet fighter flying to the left, Cordero and the other occupants of the freighter must have doubtless assumed that it was one of the planes that minutes before, had passed them at high-speed, simply because Kulyapin's plane was identical to the other four Su-15TMs that had been playing around it. Although the situation was clearly abnormal, since the presence of fighters with the Red Star undoubtedly indicated that the CL-44 was flying over territory of the Soviet Union, Cordero and Boasso should not have been assumed to have been intercepted, since the fighter did not get ahead of them nor did it flap its wings. For the rest, the Russian pilot did not wave to them either, so both must have interpreted that he was simply following them, indicating that they had deviated from the course.

For this reason, none of the Argentine pilots selected the radio on the emergency frequency of 121.5 Megahertz. If they had done so, they would have heard that they were being called insistently from the Yerevan airport, urging them to land there, although they surely would not have understood a single word since the communications were taking place in Russian, not in English, much less in Spanish. Kulyapin, for his part, had not even tried to tune in to the emergency frequency to communicate with the freighter, as this would have meant losing the essential radio link with the command post, remaining 'blind' in what was left of that already irregular procedure of interception. On the other hand, it would have been useless for him to contact the freighter pilots since he did not speak English, by now the universal language of civil aeronautical communications.

As the freighter continued to fly parallel to the border, some 40 miles inside the Soviet Union, and apparently unfazed by the fighter's presence, Kulyapin at one point asked the command post for instructions, where tempers seemed more electrified than ever. In reality, colonels Grechko and Bagdasarian did not know what to do. While for the former, the situation had become disorderly, for the latter it was still possible to get the intruder to land in Yerevan – after all, he had a fighter pilot up there flying alongside the raider. Picking up the radio, Bagdasarian personally transmitted the order to prevent the target from crossing the state border: 'Isolate him, isolate him to the border, don't give him a chance to escape'. It is most likely that by this time, the crew of the Canadair had become aware of what was happening and were trying to quickly correct their navigation error.

Hearing that the Tbilisi control centre ordered him to prevent the target from escaping across the border, Kulyapin became convinced that he was in the presence of a hostile aircraft. The command centre always had more information than the pilots in the air and besides, there were higher-ranking officers there, so there was no room for any questioning. Convinced that the freighter pilots had noticed his presence and were understanding his 'warning actions', the Russian pilot told Tbilisi that the intruder plane was not obeying his orders, which in turn, confirmed to Bagdasarian that it was an enemy aircraft, probably a spy plane or worse, a bomber disguised as a freighter.[31]

In this context of negative assumptions and misunderstandings, Commander Cordero reduced the power of his four Tyne turbines. Suddenly, the Canadair went from 620 to about 400 kilometres per hour. The deceleration was interpreted by Kulyapin as an intentional manoeuvre by the freighter pilot to force the fighter to further reduce its own speed, pushing it into a stall. In the Russian's mind, loaded with prejudices imprinted by years of political indoctrination and strict military training, there was no room to think about anything other than the hostility of the foreign pilot, even if he was in command of a heavy, four-engine cargo, ostensibly civilian and devoid of any kind of offensive or defensive weapons. To Kulyapin it was unheard of, indeed inconceivable, that this four-engine plane was even there, flying 'with impunity and arrogance' over the territory of the Soviet Union. Not for a second did he think that the crew might be lost, much less that they had been deceived by his own country's secret services.

At a certain point, the Canadair made a turn to the right, heading exactly north, at 360°, which caused real panic in Tbilisi, as it was clear that it was getting deeper and deeper into the territory of the Soviet Union. It is not clear why Commander Cordero carried out this manoeuvre. It is likely that both he and Boasso were trying to lock on some VOR or beacon that would allow them to confirm where they were, or they were simply orienting the nose of the plane with their compass reading zero and then reorienting after having defined where north was. The last contact with Ankara had required them to communicate with the Erzurum airport control tower, so they were surely trying to find that signal. Apparently, they found it, as two minutes after having headed north, the Canadair turned to the left, heading 310°. To Kulyapin, who was flying wing-to-wing, that deviation gave him the impression that the freighter was bearing down on him, and so he frantically reported it to Tiflis as he dived to avoid being collided by the Canadair. Immediately afterwards, the CL-44 took a 180° course, directly south, towards the border with Turkey, for which the Russian pilot reported three times to the control centre that 'the target was trying to escape'.[32]

A view of the Dan Accadia Hotel in Tel Aviv, on the Mediterranean coast. The photo was taken by Oscar Palacio, early in the afternoon of 18 July 1981: Palacio could not imagine that at the same time his colleagues were experiencing a major drama over Soviet Armenia. (Oscar Palacio)

In Tiflis, Bagdasarian went into a state of excitement. On the radars he had seen the erratic movement of the intruder plane, which seemed to fly freely over Azeri and Armenian territory, turning alternately to the north and south. The violation of Soviet airspace was evident, the plane did not respond to calls from the Yerevan control tower, it was clear it was a hostile aircraft, probably a decoy launched by the Americans to test how Soviet Air Defence was performing. Or even worse, a diversionary device intended to keep the fighters busy while NATO made surprise attacks on their air bases with low-flying planes. To further complicate matters, the 733 Pilot had been agitatedly reporting that the intercepted target was not following his orders, that he was carrying out dangerous manoeuvres and that he now intended to sneak across the border. Overwhelmed by all this information, Bagdasarian ordered the raider shot down, whose echo flying southward could be clearly seen on the Vozdukh-1M system displays.

Hearing the order to shoot down, Colonel Grechko was perplexed. He was the only officer at the command and control post who was aware of the secret operation planned by the KGB, whose objective was not to destroy a military plane, but to land a civilian freighter intact at some airport in the Soviet Union. Not wanting to be compromised by the impending disaster that was about to strike, Grechko hurried out of the room. Witnesses heard him murmur 'I was never here, I don't know anything at all'.[33]

Upon receiving the shoot-down order, Captain Valentin Kulyapin, in command of his Sukhoi Su-15TM fighter, asked the Soviet Union's Southern Air Defence Control Centre for confirmation. From Tbilisi, Colonel Ashot Bagdasarian's response was resounding: '733, destroy the target!' The tone and determination of the Armenian officer deeply moved the young Russian pilot. This was what he had prepared for all his life. Still shocked, he heard on the radio frequency that the control centre ordered two more fighters to take off from the Kyurdamir airfield in Azerbaijan. These were a pair of Su-15TMs led by the squadron commander, Asfar Chujo, each of which would be armed with R-98M long-range missiles equivalent to the two hanging under the wings of his own aircraft. Kulyapin immediately got into position, his mind thinking at a thousand combinations per second. To fire at the plane next to him, he had to distance himself, move at least 10 kilometres away, otherwise his firing radar would not be able to lock on to the target and the infrared seeker head of his missiles would not be able to activate either.

However, to get away he would have to turn around. At the freighter's speed, it was highly likely that by the time the fighter reached firing position, its target would have already crossed the border, as the winding Aras river was already clearly visible ahead and below. Kulyapin quickly thought that he could also withdraw from the scene and let Kyurdamir's planes fire their missiles in the distance, even from a better firing position, but this entailed the possibility of being exposed to 'friendly fire' and worst of all, it implied disobeying the demolition order he had received.[34]

He decided to put into practice the procedure in which he had been instructed to shoot down, *in extremis*, the American bombers that dared to violate the sacred airspace of the Soviet Union. The manoeuvre consisted of crashing one's own plane against the enemy plane, sectioning its tail or any of its elevators, trusting that the plane itself would continue flying after the impact.[35, 36]

Thus, while Cordero and Boasso concentrated on turning the Canadair's bow towards the Ararat River, probably checking the behaviour of the plane's VOR-DME instruments with respect to the Erzurum station at the same time, Kulyapin set about finding the best position to ram the freighter as fast as possible. He went under to the other side of the CL-44, to the right of him and went underneath. He was struck by the dirt on the freighter's belly and the enormous size of its elevators. He could see the huge propellers of the engines spinning ahead and even the grey jets of burning kerosene spewing from the great exhaust pipes of the turbines. He knew that he should not enter the turbulent vortex of the propellers, as this could shake him violently, completely out of control of his plane, which was flying at 400 kilometres per hour, almost at the limit of stall.[37]

Kulyapin got under the Canadair's tail and accelerated slowly, letting the right stabiliser go completely over his head. When he saw the blue sky light again, he let another few seconds pass, then jerked back on the joystick. The Su-15TM immediately raised its nose, as if searching for a very steep angle of climb, practically vertical and at that moment, the entire upper part of its structure, its entire back, collided abruptly with the CL-44's elevator. The fighter's glass canopy exploded from the force of the impact, sending a thousand shards of Plexiglas falling like grit onto the body of the Russian pilot, who curled into a ball in his seat.[38]

Despite the force of the blow Kulyapin did not feel any noise as he was covered by his hermetic helmet. He also did not feel the blow of the air when his cabin exploded, since he was clad in a pressurised suit that made him look like an astronaut, but he imagined that the impact against the other plane must have been strong enough to destroy his tail, so after stabilising his fighter, he judged that the mission was accomplished and decided to eject. He was in a hurry to get out of the Sukhoi because he was not sure how the plane would behave after the crash, although for the moment he kept flying without any failure, the Tumansky turbines still working perfectly. So, without even warning the Tbilisi command centre about what he had just done, he yanked on the red handles of his ejection seat.[39]

The ejection rockets were immediately activated, the cockpit bulkhead exploded upward and his seat was ejected with such speed that the acceleration rendered him momentarily unconscious. When he regained consciousness, he found himself floating in the air, hanging from the parachute, with one of his feet bare as the force of the impact against the air had torn off one of his flight boots. His chest ached, for when the blow of the wind ejected it had also ripped off a knee pad, which had struck his sternum at almost 400 kilometres per hour. He instinctively looked around and suddenly discovered the intruder plane spiralling down, probably in an unrecoverable flat spin.[40]

The last minutes of the occupants of the Canadair de TAR must have been terrifying. Without the right elevator, the plane would have pitched sharply downwards, then dipped to that side, beginning

Valentin Aleksandrovich Kulyapin, seen wearing the rank of a Captain of the V-PVO. (V-PVO)

After decorations he was promoted to major for shooting down the TAR CL-44. The Order of the Red Banner flag, the second highest medal for courage in the USSR, was awarded to him in secret because he, at least according to what Moscow explained to Buenos Aires, was dead. (V-PVO)

Years after being awarded the Order of the Red Banner for his 'feat', Kulyapin was signed out by Soviet military propaganda as an example of dedication and bravery. This presented him as shooting down a Boeing B-52 Stratofortress strategic bomber, when in fact he shot down a civilian freighter with clear civilian markings and no armament at all. Moreover, the jet he flew was a Su-15, not a MiG-21, as shown here. (V-PVO)

an endless succession of plunge turns. For Héctor Cordero and Hermete Boasso, the situation must have been desperate, unable to control a plane that was coiling downwards, approaching the limit of its structural speed, the point at which the entire structure creaks, the control surfaces become unruly and the propellers howl from the extraordinary effort it takes to be forced into a regime for which they have not been calculated. In that context, both pilots knew immediately that it would be impossible to get the old Canadair out of the crash, which had already sunk its nose well below the horizon line.

For José Burgueño and Stuart McCafferty, the situation would have been even worse, since they had no way of anticipating anything, they could not even fight with the commandos. For them it was all just feeling the plane fall, the sun appearing at regular intervals in the same window, the brown earth and the blue sky alternating as each corkscrew turn was completed, each time faster. All of the items in Compartment B, all of the galley supplies and all of the objects in the cockpit, flew through the air and ended up smashed against the left internal wall due to the centrifugal force of the spins. At one point, the pressure must have been such that it left the four occupants unconscious. It was a blessing from God, for they felt nothing when the 50-tonne plane crashed violently into the side of a granite mountain in Armenia, just three miles from the Turkish border.

The drama was witnessed from the ground by Turkish soldiers and officers stationed in front of the Soviet border, who could see how the large four-engine plane fell like a burning torch, while the smaller jet disappeared behind the hills, also engulfed in flames. until it fell into a swamp full of reeds. The Canadair fragmented from the force of the impact against the mountain, scattering its wreckage for several hundred metres in all directionsand caught fire. The Su-15, by contrast, plunged like a supersonic dagger into the mud. It left a huge circular hole that immediately covered the muddy water.[41]

General Zavitsky (centre), member of the second Soviet investigation commission sent from Moscow to unravel what happened to the TAR CL-44. He confirmed that at the time it was shot-down, the aircraft was underway without cargo on board. (V-PVO)

The disappearance of the Argentine freighter triggered the search, assistance and rescue (SAR) procedure provided for in Annex 12 of the International Civil Aviation Convention, which air traffic services around the world must activate in cases of disappearance or presumed accident of a civil aircraft. Half an hour after losing radio contact with the Canadair CL-44 that was flying from Iran, the Ankara control centre launched the first alert, which was confirmed when the plane did not reach its planned destination on the island of Cyprus. In this phase of uncertainty, the rescue coordination centre was summoned, which in this case depended on the Turkish Air Force since the plane's last contact had been with Turkish air traffic controllers.[42]

Senior officers of the 166th Fighter Aviation Regiment during a ceremony held at the Sandar AB, on occasion of awarding the Order of the Red Banner to Major Valentin Kulyapin, in November 1981. (V-PVO)

Consultations with the Armenian air traffic services soon confirmed that the missing plane had not landed at Zvarnots, giving rise to reasonable indications that it might be in distress. From then on, the SAR service of Turkey tried by all means to determine the location of the freighter, reporting the disappearance to the aircraft operating company (Afro Continental), to the State of Registry (the Argentine Republic), to the air traffic units throughout Turkey, to the rescue coordination centres of all contiguous states (Iran, Iraq, Cyprus and the Soviet Union) and to the Turkish aircraft accident investigation authorities, with whom an action plan was coordinated to initiate search and rescue operations.

СООБЩЕНИЕ ТАСС

18 июля 1981 г. самолет неустановленной принадлежности со стороны Ирана вошел в воздушное пространство Советского Союза в районе города Еревана.

На все запросы советских наземных служб контроля за полетами самолетов и попытки оказания ему помощи экипаж самолета не отвечал, продолжал полет над советской территорией, совершая при этом опасные маневрирования.

Через некоторое время этот самолет столкнулся с советским самолетом, разрушился и сгорел.

The press release issued by the Soviet TASS News Agency; the only official information provided by Moscow in reaction to the downing of the Argentine CL-44. The text read: 'On 18 July 1981, an aircraft of unestablished ownership entered from Iran into the airspace of the USSR in the area of Yerevan. All the attempts to establish communication by the ground control and aircraft remained unanswered, and the aircraft continued flying over the Soviet territory, carrying out dangerous manoeuvres at the same time. After a while, the said aircraft collided with a Soviet aircraft, crashed, and caught fire.' (TASS)

The news of the disappearance of the Canadair was officially communicated by the Turkish Air Force to the Argentine Air Force during the night of 18 to 19 July 1981. The information arrived by teletype on the tenth floor of the Condor Building, where the Communications Department was located and was received by Captain Armando Elio Buira, who was the officer in charge of the night watch. A few hours later, Jack Malloch communicated the news to Robert Harte, the commercial manager of the Swiss cargo company Transvalair, the commercial representative that TAR had at Basel Airport. At six in the morning on Sunday 19 July 1981, Transvalair transmitted the news by telex to the TAR headquarters in Buenos Aires, which received the news at 11 in the morning due to the time difference between Switzerland and Argentina.[43]

What followed was a true diplomatic siege from the Argentine government to the Soviet government, to find out what had happened to the Argentine plane and its crew. On Friday 31 July 1981, 13 days after the disappearance of the Canadair, the Moscow government finally authorised the Argentine Ambassador to the Soviet Union, Leopoldo Bravo, to visit the site of the accident, for which he set a date for Monday 3 August. Bravo immediately

José María Paletta, Operations Manager of Transporte Aéreo Rioplatense, explaining to the press the details of the disappearance of the Canadair CL-44 with registration LV-JTN, at the company's offices, on 22 July 1981. 'The aircraft was hired by a foreign company to make a charter flight transporting medicine and food products from Larnaca to Tehran'. (La Semana)

Andrei Gromyko, Minister of Foreign Affairs of the USSR at the time of the disappearance of the Argentine CL-44. The absolute master of Soviet diplomacy, he was known for his skill, thoroughness and intransigence. That he had authorised the inspection of the crash site, can be considered a major achievement of Argentine diplomacy. (Guido Ghiretti collection)

The Undersecretary of Foreign Relations Jorge Enrique Ros (Guido Ghiretti collection)

Ambassador of the Argentine Republic to the Union of the Soviet Socialist Republics, Leopoldo Bravo. Both men exerted unprecedented diplomatic pressure on the government in Moscow in an attempt to clarify the circumstances in which the TAR freighter had disappeared. (Guido Ghiretti collection)

The site where the CL-44 Swingtail of the TAR crashed, as seen by Ambassador Leopoldo Bravo, Commodore Rodolfo Echegoyen and Consular Secretary Silvia Mira. (Ruslan Altimirov, via Valentin Kulyapin)

Wreckage of one of Rolls-Royce Tyne turbines, with its Dowty propeller. (Ruslan Altimirov, via Valentin Kulyapin)

Wreckage of the aircraft fuselage. Bravo, Echegoyen and Mira dedicated themselves to rummaging through the debris to find parts that had serial numbers that could help identify the aircraft. Before long, it became clear this was the Swingtail of the TAR. (Ruslan Altimirov, via Valentin Kulyapin)

reported the news to the Argentine Foreign Ministry, requesting authorisation to make the trip with the Embassy's Aeronautical and Naval Attaché (Comodoro Rodolfo Echegoyen) and the Head of the Consular Section (Silvia Mira). The authorisation was granted on 1 August by secret cable sent by Minister Guillermo Conti, Head of the Eastern Europe Department, who insisted on the need to have official information on the facts. Likewise, and at the request of the Argentine Air Force, Conti required Bravo to request from the Soviet authorities, the aircraft's flight and voice parameter recorders, as well as 'all other information of interest related to said flight and subsequent accident'. The allusion to an 'accident' on the part of the Air Force denoted the will to obtain information for the purposes of the investigation by the Civil Aviation Accident Investigation Board (JIACA) which at that time, depended on the Air Regions Command of that Force.[44]

On Monday 3 August 1981, at 08:00 a.m., Ambassador Bravo, Commodore Etchegoyen, and Consular Secretary Mira left Domodedovo International Airport in a Tupolev Tu-134 airliner specially rented by the Soviet government to take them to the city of Yerevan, at a cost of 5,000 roubles. They reached their destination at 11:45 a.m. local time (10:45 a.m. Moscow time), after a 2:40-hour flight. At the Zvartnots airport, a delegation of about 10 people was waiting for them, headed by the Deputy Minister of Armenia, Serguei

Simonian and by the representative of the USSR Civil Aviation entity, Alexei Smirnov. The Argentines had no way of knowing that Smirnov was not who he claimed to be, but an Aviation Colonel General appointed secretly by the Council of Ministers of the Soviet Union to chair the commission of inquiry created by Soviet Premier Leonid Brezhnev, with the purpose of knowing what happened on 18 July 1981 over the skies of Armenia. His presence at the head of the team that would receive the Argentine diplomats was not aimed at clarifying anything, but rather at obstructing their investigations as much as possible, thus consolidating the alibi of a merely accidental air collision between the Canadair CL-44 and the Su-15TM. Moreover, the Minister of Civil Aviation of the Soviet Union, Ivan Stepanovich Silaev, never found out that a 'representative' of his organisation was working in Armenia.[45]

9

SHADOWS UPON SHADOWS

The delegation of Argentines, Russians and Armenians went to the place where the accident had occurred, some 50km southeast of the city of Yerevan, transferring to special vehicles due to the difficulties of access to the site. Upon reaching about 500 metres from the wreckage, a large dark spot of about 60 metres in diameter could be observed, almost on the top of a hill 1,300 metres high. From there, the officials had to climb a distance of 400 metres with a slope of 60 degrees, to reach the accident site.[1]

It was here that the charred remains of the Canadair CL-44 could be seen, scattered in a circle approximately 50 metres in diameter. Among the debris, it was possible to identify the four engines with their respective propellers, part of the main landing gear, pieces of the cabin and segments of the main planes and the empennage. Various pieces were located that undoubtedly, allowed to infer the identity of the device, such as a Kidde brand oxygen cylinder, a Parker brand low-pressure fuel valve, a Glendale Instrument Corp brand instrument, a Browline brand cargo securing hook and a primed part with the number 44D-50752, which directly alluded to the manufacturer of the plane, Canadair Limited. After three hours of inspection, the delegation returned to Yerevan, heading to the Central Hospital morgue, where the remains of Héctor Cordero, Hermete Boasso and José Burgueño were deposited, whose recognition was impossible since the bodies were completely charred.[2]

The ceremony and the act of cremation of the bodies took place on Wednesday 5 August 3:45 p.m., at the Moscow City Crematorium. Ambassador Bravo requested that the Funeral March be conducted on the occasion and that the voluntary presence of the Argentine colony linked to his embassy, be allowed to attend. Twelve Argentines and four Soviets attended the cremation. The urns with the ashes were delivered the next day to Commodore Echegoyen by Minister Gennady Sazhenev (official of the USSR Ministry of Foreign Affairs) and by Sergei Frantsev (representative of the USSR Ministry of Civil Aviation). The three urns with the documentation proving the death and cremation of their owners were shipped on the first commercial Aeroflot flight that departed for Paris and from there to Buenos Aires on Aerolíneas Argentinas flight 133, which arrived at Ezeiza at 9:00 a.m. on the morning of 10 August 1981. Commodore Rodolfo Echegoyen was travelling with the three boxes, in charge of delivering them and formalising the paperwork required by the Ministry of Foreign Affairs.[3]

As for Captain Valentin Kulyapin, although his performance in the process of intercepting the Argentine plane had been a real disaster, his decoration was promoted due to the manifest courage he had shown in complying with the shoot-down order that had been issued to him. However, as the target had turned out to be a civil plane, not a military one, he would not be awarded the title of Hero of the Soviet Union but the medal corresponding to the Order of the Red Banner, the second in importance and hierarchy. By order of the Presidium of the Supreme Soviet of the Soviet Union, Kulyapin was decorated on 29 September 1981 in a secret ceremony, since the Argentine government was informed that he had died in the air collision. His status as bearer of the Order of the Red Banner was communicated to the 166th Fighter Aviation Regiment in November of that year, giving rise to a closed formation in the barracks. It was necessary to show examples of dedication and heroism to the new generations of Soviet officers, even more so considering that at any moment the unit would deploy to Afghanistan, where the war had been going on for two years and the casualties were increasing.[4, 5, 6]

Kulyapin's decoration was not the only action the Soviet Union kept secret, the entire operation to shoot down the Argentine freighter was contained under lock and key. Israel and Iran did the same so as not to reveal the arms traffic that they were conducting

The then-Captain Marat Syrtlanov (centre) – a paratrooper and war correspondent of the Soviet Armed Forces – talks with a young soldier in Afghanistan. His in-depth investigations soon brought him face-to-face with the cover-up that the Soviet government had perpetrated around the shoot-down of the Argentine CL-44. (Marat Syrtlanov)

Colonel Marat Syrtlanov, a veteran of the wars in Afghanistan and Chechnya, had the intellectual honesty and civic courage to reveal the cover-up that the government of the Soviet Union had perpetrated regarding the downing of the Transport Aéreo Rioplatense aircraft. (Marat Syrtlanov)

with each other, while the United States kept absolute silence about what happened. If the supply of North American weapons to Iran was aired, the self-violation of the embargo would be exposed. The Argentine government, for its part, decided to throw a cloak of oblivion over everything that had happened so as not to sour its relations with the Soviet Union, by far the main destination for its grain exports. The downing of the LV-JTN thus became a true Cold War crime covered up by five states. The details only came to light long after the democratic opening in Argentina.[7]

The most illuminating documents of that demolition, such as the end of the companies Aerotransportes Entre Ríos and TAR, would only be discovered on 31 October 2013, during the maintenance tasks contracted by the Argentine Air Force in the subsoil of its headquarters, the Condor Building, located at Avenida Pedro Zanni 250, in the Retiro neighbourhood of Buenos Aires. The workers in charge found dozens of bookcases neatly arranged on the shelves of a three-metre-long by two-metre-high cabinet, plus two heavy safes and two closets. As it was necessary to remove it all to continue working, the foreman asked what to do with the furniture and stationery. When the Air Force officers in charge of supervising the work went in to review the files and to find out whether or not its contents justified throwing it away, they were stunned. Each library was full of reserved, confidential and secret documents generated during the seven years of the National Reorganisation Process, the de facto government that had governed the country between 1976 and 1983. Inside the strongboxes, there were 280 records of secret meetings held by the Military Government Junta and the originals of the notorious 'black lists' of intellectuals, artists and journalists that the dictatorship had tried to silence during the 'years of lead'.[8]

The mere existence of so many documents, so neatly safeguarded, was in itself a surprising discovery given that the last months of the Process had been characterised by the burning of sensitive or compromising files; a systematic mechanism that occurred in all the units and dependencies of the armed forces, but particularly those that had been most committed to the 'dirty war'. It was striking that so many revealing pieces of paper could have survived the burning and even more so, considering that most of them could have been suppressed by the Air Force without arousing any suspicion. The Air Force could simply have claimed that they disappeared in the eight-storey collapse suffered by the south wing of the Condor Building on a rainy afternoon of 5 December 1980, as a result of which four people died and another 18 were injured.[9]

As soon as he became aware of the discovery of the documents, the Chief of the General Staff of the Air Force, Brigadier Major Mario Miguel Callejo, informed the Minister of Defence of the Nation, Agustín Rossi. The basement of the Condor Building was immediately sealed by the Secretary for Strategies and Military Affairs (Jorge Fernández), the Undersecretary for Strategic Planning and Military Policy (Fernanda Llobet), the General Director of Legal Affairs and the National Director of Human Rights and International Law Humanitarian. Immediately afterwards, the minister authorised the declassification tasks and in less than 24 hours, a team of 12 people assigned by the National Human Rights Secretariat, joined the work.

Due to the conditions of the subsoil, it was decided to transfer the documentation to another Air Force building. While the move began, the Minister of Defence issued Resolution MD No. 445/13 instructing the Chief of the Joint Staff and the Chiefs of the General Staff of the three armed forces, to exhaustively relieve in all the dependencies corresponding to their agencies, sites where there may be documentation or information of legal interest, including, especially, those not intended for filing, custody or storage. The Resolution also established that the working group on archives, coordinated by the National Directorate of Human Rights and International Humanitarian Law, would be in charge of carrying out the tasks of preservation and identification for the preparation of an inventory of the documentary collection found, in a six month period.

By the time the work was finished, two documentary collections were perfectly classified, the first corresponding to the archive of the General Secretariat of the Air Force and the second belonging to the Shift Secretariat of the Military Junta, which in December 1983 was in charge of the Air Force. The so-called Open Archives were in charge of the Directorate of Historical Studies of the Argentine Air Force (with headquarters at Calle Viamonte 153, on the south side of the Alas Building), given its mission to gather, preserve, investigate, register and preserve the assets documentaries that constitute the aeronautical cultural historical heritage of the Argentine Republic. A consultation terminal for the Open Archives was set up at the National Aeronautics Library, located on the third floor of Calle Paraguay 748, Autonomous City of Buenos Aires.

The declassification of documents derived from the Open Archives programme was essential to understand the treatment given by the Argentine government to the demolition in Armenia of the Canadair CL-44 of TAR and even the details surrounding the operation of the company during the last years of the government military. The discovery of the documents made it possible to confirm that, contrary to all that could be imagined, the loss of the LV-JTN was not a coup de grace for TAR. It was a hard economic blow but the company fully collected the hull insurance contracted with La Universal, which at the same time recovered the payment through the National Reinsurance Institute (INDER). Although it is true that the money resulting from the compensation was not applied to the replacement of the plane, this did not mean that the company was affected operationally, since it still led the Canadair CL-44 fleet integrated with Aerotransportes Entre Ríos and still better, it still had two Boeing 707 freighter jets. For this reason, it could be said that at the end of 1981, while the Argentine economy was sinking into a vortex of galloping inflation, TAR exhibited a remarkable state of health, since practically all its contracts were concluded in dollars and a good part of its cargo operation arrangements were made directly abroad and with foreign clients.

Apparently, this atypical boom situation put the company under a shadow of dark interests. In February 1982, seven months after the disappearance of the LV-JTN, the president of the company, Carlos Martínez Guerrero, was contacted by Antonio Corigliano, a 53 year-old businessman who owned the commercial firm A. Corigliano SA. and shareholder in Compañía Constructora Latinoamericana SA and in the firm Centro Regional Noreste SRL.[10,, 11,, 12]

Corigliano did not come from the aeronautical field at all, he had no experience in air transport and until the moment of contacting Martínez Guerrero he worked 'as a controller for the entry of vegetables into the Central Market'. Two sources consulted indicate that, in reality, Corigliano was a figurehead for the Chief of the General Staff of the Argentine Air Force, Brigadier Major Basilio Lami Dozo, the Secretary General of the institution, Brigadier Rodolfo Aquilino Guerra and Commodore Guillermo Sebastián Palacio, who had retired from active service on 31 December 1980. One of these sources goes even further, indicating that Lami Dozo and Guerra exerted direct influence on the Minister of Economy of the Nation, Roberto Teodoro Alemann, 'to put pressure on Mr. Carlos Martínez Guerrero, causing him to finally hand over the company TAR to the so-called Mr. Corigliano without payment of any kind'.[13, 14]

Although these accusations were never proven and although it is possible to presume honour in every officer of the Argentine Air Force, the context and the results allow some support to be given to these versions, mainly due to the enormous power held by Brigadiers Lami Dozo and Guerra in a period of Argentine history, in which the rule of law had been fractured.

Brigadier Rodolfo Aquilino Guerra had been appointed Secretary General of the Air Force on 17 March 1981, after having previously served as an aeronautical attaché at the Argentine Embassy in London between 1976 and 1978. He was a tough man, a skilful operator and a staunch anti-Peronist; with the rank of Lieutenant, he had integrated the group of officers of the VII Air Brigade that on 16 June 1955, had revolted against the constitutional government of President Perón, later fleeing to Uruguay. [15, 16, 17]

For his part, Brigadier Lami Dozo was a man with an extremely low profile and almost no public exposure. He had served since 1975 as Chief I of the General Staff of the Argentine Air Force, then as Secretary General and finally, as Commander of Air Operations. He had been promoted to Brigadier General and appointed Commander-in-Chief of the force on Thursday 17 December 1981, when Brigadier General Omar Domingo Rubens Graffigna decided to advance the delivery of the Aeronautics command by one month.[18,, 19]

Lami Dozo's power was immeasurable and measured by democratic standards, arguably excessive. In accordance with the organic structure of the National Reorganisation Process, his access to the Commander-in-Chief of the Air Force had ensured him one of the three seats in the Military Junta that had governed the country since 24 March 1976. This plainly meant that it held a third of the de facto political power, with direct interference in all levels of the state organisation chart and territorial control in six Argentine jurisdictions (Federal Capital, Entre Ríos, La Rioja, Mendoza, San Luis and Santa Cruz), as such had been the distribution agreed with the Army and the Navy after the coup d'état.[20]

Lami Dozo became the highest authority of the Argentine Air Force at a time when the said institution held the greatest military power in its history, with nine fully equipped Air Brigades, a Military Aircraft Factory in full production, a school of model aviation, development of space technology and even an ongoing top-secret missile project. In addition to this combat capacity, polished in innumerable verification operations and duly equipped for the frustrated war with Chile in 1978, the Air Force held total and absolute control of the Argentine Civil Aviation, from the representation of the country before the Organisation of International Civil Aviation, to the administration of air traffic radars. This also included the qualification of aerodromes, the granting of licences to personnel, the registration of all types of aircraft, the granting of authorisations for commercial use, the investigation of aviation accidents and the qualification of factories and aeronautical workshops, these are examples of just some of the most relevant functions or activities. In this context, the fact that Brigadiers Lami Dozo and Guerra kept an eye on TAR was not a minor fact at all.

Among the civil aeronautical organisations over which Lami Dozo exercised control, the Sociedad del Estado Aerolíneas Argentinas stood out, which had always been the natural destination for many retired military pilots who wanted to remain active in the commercial aviation field after passing through the Argentine Air Force. Since October 1968, Aerolíneas Argentinas had been operating two Boeing 707-387C with dual capacity for transporting passengers and cargo, since they had a front door that made them suitable for this second role. Aerolíneas had made little or no use of the capacities of both freighters, largely because this meant going out to look for clients instead of simply waiting for them to show up at their agencies and commercial offices, as they were used to doing with their thousands of passengers. However, starting in 1976, and under the control of Vice Commodore Roberto Vicente Martorano (until 1979) and retired Brigadier Major Pablo Osvaldo Apella (since 1979), the state company gradually increased the volumes of cargo transported, reducing the idle capacity of its warehouses on the international routes that it was authorised to exploit. Thus, Aerolíneas Argentinas went from transporting 74 million tons/km in 1975 to some 192 million tons/km in 1980.[21]

Since the operating costs of the two mixed Boeing 707s were supported by the income from the air tickets paid by the passengers, Aerolíneas Argentinas began to sell cargo transfers at ridiculously low rates and even below the market price, a luxury that could happen because it was not a true commercial company forced to generate profits, but a state company whose continuous deficit was covered by the public treasury. This predatory commercial behaviour of Airlines increased from December 1981, when the third Military Junta, made up of Brigadier General Basilio Lami Dozo, came to power. From that moment onwards, the state company completely converted its two mixed Boeing 707s to the role of pure freighters, generating unfair competition for TAR, with which it was very difficult to coexist. The conversion of the Boeing airlines could be a mere unfortunate coincidence that occurred at a time when Antonio Corigliano approached to negotiate with Carlos Martínez Guerrero, the purchase of the share package of TAR; alternatively, it could be compliance with the order given by someone from the highest spheres of the Condor Building. Whatever the case, the result was the same; the private company was obliged to accept the new rules imposed by Airlines and could not complain at all to the National Directorate of Air Transport Commercial at the risk of seeing its claim rejected and in addition, being administratively persecuted by an Air Force that exercised control of the airworthiness of its aircraft.[22]

In this context, TAR doubled its commercial efforts in the country and sought to remain current in the competitive international market, flying in many cases without touching Argentine soil, under the protection of the Fifth Freedom of the air rights enshrined in the

International Civil Aviation Agreement. Basically, the situation was extremely unfair (and even perverse) because while TAR was forced to generate profits at the risk of going into default or bankruptcy, Aerolíneas was happily supported by a national budget that was integrated, among many other incomes, with the taxes paid by TAR, the private company against which it was competing.

Along with Brigadier Basilio Lami Dozo, the triad of the Military Junta that came to power on 22 December 1981, included Lieutenant General Leopoldo Fortunato Galtieri and Admiral Jorge Isaac Anaya. It was the third triumvirate since the military coup of 1976 and by far, the most conflictive of all due to the state of decomposition that the national economy had been exhibiting. Galtieri belonged to the hardest wing of the Army and during the National Reorganisation Process, he had served as Commander of the Army's II and I Corps and as Commander-in-Chief of that force since December 1979. For his part, Anaya had been Director General of the Naval Personnel and Director General of Naval Instruction, Chief of the Naval Staff and Commander-in-Chief of the Navy as of September 1981. Anaya was a fervent nationalist, a staunch anti-communist and a potential bellicose. Even before he took office as a member of the Military Junta on 22 December 1981, he gave precise instructions to initiate an old Navy plan, which was the military recovery of the Malvinas Islands.

Galtieri bought the idea immediately, seeing in it the possibility of revitalising the government of the Process through the popular support that a patriotic feat of this magnitude would produce. Lami Dozo objected to the plan as soon as he was informed, but he could not go against the will of the Army and the Navy, largely because Galtieri and Anaya were friends and had known each other since their first years of training at the National Military College. On Tuesday 26 January 1982, at 9:00 a.m., the Military Junta met in the Libertad Building, headquarters of the Argentine Navy. On the occasion, the National Strategy Directive (DENAC) No. 1/82 was issued, where it was established as a political objective 'to consolidate Argentine sovereignty in the Malvinas, Georgias and South Sandwich Islands and contribute to affirming its full exercise in the South Atlantic'.[23]

Admiral Anaya, Lieutenant-General Galtieri and Brigadier General Lami Dozo during the trial to which they were submitted in 1985, for their responsibility during the National Reorganisation Process. (TELAM)

Since the beginning of the National Reorganisation Process, the state company Aerolinas Argentinas progressively increased its participation in the cargo transportation segment. For this purpose, it deployed its two freighters Boeing 707-387C (this photograph is showing one of them, registered as LV-JGR). The unequal competition with TAR became particularly tough when Brigadier General Basilio Lami Dozo became the Chief-of-Staff of the Argentine Air Force. (Guido Ghiretti collection)

For the Military Junta, the strategy was summed up by occupying the Malvinas Islands militarily in an absolutely bloodless manner and withdrawing immediately afterwards to negotiate sovereignty with the United Kingdom of Great Britain. All Argentine government analysts agreed that the British would limit themselves to ignoring the fact, formally protesting to Argentina by withdrawing their Ambassador from Buenos Aires or else breaking diplomatic relations (imposing some diplomatic sanctions as well). On no account was the possibility of a British military response being considered. The entire conflict hypothesis was based, then, on the fact that there would be no conflict. However, the Junta would produce a significant deployment of military forces to Patagonia because, as soon as the issue of Argentine sovereignty over the Malvinas was resolved, an attack would be launched on Chilean territory to decide by arms, the border dispute over three islands located in the Beagle Channel, in the far south of both Countries. [24]

Between dawn and the early hours of the morning of 2 April 1982, tactical divers and regular troops of the Argentine Marine Infantry landed in the Malvinas

Islands as part of Operation Azul, the amphibious segment of Operation Rosario, a complex operation by which the military occupation of the archipelago would take place. When the news was communicated to the country, millions of Argentines vibrant with patriotism, filled the streets of all towns and cities, expressing never-before-seen feelings of national unity and producing the long-awaited wave of support for the government, which the Military Junta had planned since the first moment. However, contrary to what Argentine analysts and diplomats expected, the UK government reacted immediately to the invasion. On the same 2 April while crowds cheered de facto President Galtieri in the Plaza de Mayo, British Prime Minister Margaret Thatcher convened her emergency cabinet and approved the deployment of a task force to recover the islands. Nine Royal Navy warships conducting manoeuvres in the Mediterranean were immediately headed for the South Atlantic. On 3 April, the first elements of the Royal Air Force were deployed to Ascension Island and two days later, the bulk of the British fleet, led by the aircraft carriers HMS *Hermes* and HMS *Invincible*, left Portsmouth harbour.[25]

The possibility of open war with Great Britain, which had not even entered the minds of the most daring 'planners' in the armed forces, became a tangible reality in Buenos Aires. At that precise moment, Argentina faced two realities. The first, that it urgently needed weapons and spare parts to face what was coming and the second, half of the world's markets had been closed to Argentina for having declared war on a nuclear potential that also had a permanent seat on the Security Council of the United Nations Organisation.

On 30 April 1982 Great Britain declared a total exclusion zone of 200 nautical miles around the Falkland Islands, announcing that any ship or aircraft of any nationality entering the sector could be attacked without warning. That same day, Carlos Martínez Guerrero handed over the share package in TAR to the presumed front men of Brigadiers Basilio Lami Dozo and Rodolfo Aquilino Guerra. The transfer was signed by Stewart Robbins, José Lucio Guerrero and Antonio Corigliano, who from then on, held the shares that until now had been owned by Martínez Guerrero, Gloria Susana González Howard de Martínez Guerrero, Armando Tola, Carlos Federico Martínez Guerrero, Ernesto Maxwell Wood, Roberto Botti, Carlos Pastor Baldassarre, Luis Lennart Curt Schenstrom, Guillermo Enrique Martínez Guerrero, Celia Anzoátegui de Serilieper and Guillermo Roque González Howard. The new board of directors of the company was made up of Antonio Corigliano (President), Stewart Robbins (Vice President) and José Lucio Guerrero (Titular Director). The trustees were Drs. Carlos V. Branchini and Ramona Francisca Pane de Petraglia. The transfer of TAR's share package was authorised by the National Secretary of Finance, Engineer Manuel Solané and by Commodore Horacio Larghi, National Director of Commercial Air Transport.[26 27 28]

According to the new conformation, 72 percent of the original shares of TAR remained in the hands of Antonio Corigliano, while the remaining 20 percent became the property of Stewart Robbins, who was a representative of North American investors whose identity has not been revealed. However, a consulted source refers to George Batchelor, the king of air transport in Miami, who by then had a stake in more than 40 cargo companies, directly or through his companies International Air Lease Incorporated and Aero Finance Incorporated.[29, 30]

The new owners stated that TAR would no longer carry out flights to Europe, limiting itself to expanding its influence in the inter-American markets, especially the United States, using the two Boeing 707s plus a Canadair CL-44 that at that time was undergoing an intense general tour in Miami workshops. Apparently, the decision to leave the European market was a direct consequence of the Falklands War, since one of TAR's main trading partners was a British company, Transmeridian Air Cargo. On 2 April 1982, the same as the occupation of the archipelago, the Bank of England decided to freeze 1,400 million Argentine dollars deposited in British banks. Argentina responded to these trade sanctions by freezing British assets in the country, prohibiting the importation of products manufactured in the United Kingdom and suspending all types of payments to English banks. In this context, it was very difficult to transfer to Buenos Aires, any profit generated through Transmeridian, so TAR simply decided to withdraw from the European market. It was a risky measure from a commercial point of view since, at that time, the company accumulated debts with foreign suppliers for US$3,072,166, debts with national suppliers for $4,861,644,244, plus social, fiscal and social security debts for more than 1,500 million pesos.[31, 32, 33]

On 1 May 1982, one day after the transfer of the shareholding package of TAR and less than a month after the Argentine occupation of the Malvinas, an AVRO Vulcan strategic bomber from the Royal Air Force and BAE Sea Harrier fighters from the embarked component of the fleet, bombarded the Port Stanley airport (renamed 'Puerto Argentino' after the invasion) and the Goose Green airfield (renamed 'Pradera del Ganso'). The Falklands War, which should never have started, ended much earlier than expected with a painful Argentine defeat. On 14 June 1982, 74 days after the occupation, the Argentine forces presented their surrender in the archipelago. The news fell came as a shock to the Argentine population, who until then, had been convinced of victory due to the successful information that the official statements had been providing. When the defeat became apparent, the same people who had cheered in the Plaza de Mayo on the unforgettable 2 April, rose in riots in the same square, demanding the heads of those responsible. The de facto government entered a climate of true chaos. Lieutenant General Galtieri resigned from the Military Junta on 17 June 1982, two months later Brigadier General Basilio Lami Dozo retired and on 1 October 1982, Admiral Anaya was replaced.

Starting in February 1982, the President of the TAR, Carlos Martínez Guerrero, came under severe pressure to get rid of the company. He ended the affair on 30 April 1982, when handing over his shares to Antonio Corigliano, who would have been the 'front man' for Brigadier General Basilio Lami Dozo, then the Chief-of-Staff of the Argentine Air Force. (Horacio Víctor Franco)

By that time, it was clear that the National Reorganisation Process had come to an end, so the last de facto president, General Reynaldo Bignone, began the path of transition to democracy. The elections were held on 30 October 1983 and the new constitutional president, Dr. Raúl Alfonsín, took office on 10 December of that same year.

On 22 November 1982, when Brigadiers Lami Dozo and Guerra had already formally left their positions in the Condor Building, Brigadier José María Insúa, Chief of the General Staff of the Argentine Air Force, sent to the new Minister of Economy of the Nación, Dr. Jorge Wehbe, a note of support for the request that TAR had presented. It was for the refinancing of the debts that the company maintained for loans with the Banco de la Nación Argentina (USD 10,131,400) and for fallen guarantees with the Ministry of Economy itself ($26,982,015,470). The note stated that TAR was 'the only private Argentine international air cargo company', that it did not have state subsidies of any kind and that it was evident that if it obtained a refinancing of its liabilities, it would be able to meet its obligations and also become a profitable company of national capital. In the words of Brigadier Insúa:

> [...] It is demonstrated that this company, maintaining its current management style and having official support based on the refinancing of its debt with the Ministry of Economy and Banco Nación, can not only maintain sources of work but also develop for the country a national capital company with international impact.
>
> This Air Force asks that Ministry to see fit, within its powers, to provide the support requested by the TAR company. This is necessary because the existence of national flag air warehouses is going through a stage that is estimated to be transitory, of excess supply due to the simultaneous drop in our country of exports and exports, a fact that has not been common in the past.[34]

It was obvious that the Air Force was lobbying in favour of TAR at a time when the National Reorganisation Process was going through its last months of existence, this would elliptically confirm the control exercised behind the scenes by the now retired Brigadiers, Lami Dozo and Guerra. The intercession before the Ministry of Economy was kept strictly confidential and all the documents that evidenced it were kept in the secret file in the basement of the Condor Building, out of any official inventory and away from any prying eye.[35]

The transfer of the share package of TAR, processed in file 1,608,749 of the Air Force, was definitively approved on 22 February 1983 by Decree of the National Executive Branch No. 438/83 signed by the de facto President of the Nation, General Reynaldo Bignone. From then on, although it continued to fly, it progressively reduced its capital and its real operating capacities.

On 29 December 1988, five years after the transfer of the shareholding package of TAR had taken place, a complaint prepared by the so-called Anonymous Investigative Commission for the denunciation of illegal acts, began to circulate in the newsrooms of the main specialised media in the country, against the nation. It was a multi-page document in which 'the true story of TAR' was told and

A notice published in 1987 by Transporte Aéreo Rioplatense, adhering to the 75th Anniversary of the Argentine Air Force. There could be no better endorsement of its control by officials from the latter institution, given that no private company could have spent money on an announcement to greet this occasion. (Pablo Potenze collection)

The Boeing 707-338C with registration LV-MZE (named 'San Jorge') as seen already with turbines and landing gear removed, while waiting to be scrapped at the Miami International, on 22 October 1993 – by this time, Transporte Aéreo Rioplatense had already been declared bankrupt. (Eduardo Perusquia)

appealing to the recipients to investigate or file the corresponding criminal complaints. The text abounded in detail regarding allegedly criminal conduct by Antonio Corigliano, including tax fraud, credit fraud, fraudulent administration, asset sales contrary to the interests of the company and the Bank of the Argentine Nation and business account emptying. The complaint stated that the Commission should carry out its activity in anonymity 'in order not to generate reprisals or preventive judicial resources that could defeat its objective: to promote the imprisonment of the Nation's fraudsters'.

The Anonymous Commission had little commission and also little anonymity. From a simple reading of the complaint, it was perfectly inferred that the pen behind the text was that of Carlos Martínez Guerrero, who was most likely, seconded only by his wife, Gloria González Howard. According to the complaint, immediately after the transfer of the share package to Antonio Corigliano took place, TAR began to use 'abusively and indiscriminately' the tax forms that allowed it to transfer funds abroad, 'managing in this way to obtain exchange differences on false invoices worth several million dollars'. In the months that followed, the company sold two and a half million dollars' worth of 'CL-44 aircraft spare parts that were in the Ezeiza hangars and that were sent abroad for undocumented sale' and for half a million of dollars, 'CL-44 aircraft engines that were at the Rolls-Royce factory in Canada, which were part of the mortgage inventory of Banco de la Nación and whose sale was never documented in real values'.

The four turbines of the Boeing 707 LV-MSG and the inertial navigation equipment of the Boeing 707 LV-MZE had also been sold, the latter acquired by the Argentine Air Force at a rate of $120,000 each. Finally, TAR had stopped paying the Banco de la Nación Argentina all the instalments of a credit previously granted for 11 million dollars, although there had been no claim in the face of non-compliance because 'the Ministry of Economy was promptly raising each instalment, in its capacity as guarantor of the credit'.[36]

Although full credit cannot be given to an anonymous complaint, the context and other sources consulted allow to infer the veracity of the information, since as of May 1982, not only the emptying

Canadair CL-44 Swingtail with registration LV-JZM, seen at the start of the scrapping process, in front of the hangar of the Transporte Aéreo Rioplatense in Ezeiza. Notably, the Number 2 Rolls-Royce Tyne turbine has already been removed. (Gabriel Pavlovcic collection, via José Cheja)

The same aircraft, already without engines and propellers (and probably, with all of its cockpit instrumentation removed), as seen at Ezeiza, at the start of its 'cannibalisation' process. Notably, under the Argentine flag on the fin, there was also the title Argentina, which its twin LV-JTN did not have. The clear identification of the country of registration was one of the lessons learned by the company through the tragic downing of the LV-JTN. (Enrique Abeiedo via Michael Magnusson)

The Canadair CL-44 Swingtail with registration LV-JZM – a 'twin' of the LV-JTN –seen at Chivatos sector of the Ezeiza International in 1988, awaiting its final fate in form of the scrapper's torch, already without propellers or engines. (Guido Chiretti collection)

and liquidation of TAR was verified, but also that of its company associate, Aerotransportes Entre Ríos, whose share package had also been acquired by Antonio Corigliano.[37]

Indeed, in May 1982, shortly after Carlos Martínez Guerrero parted with his shareholding in TAR, the Canadair CL-44D Swingtail registration LV-JZM, was taken out of service and dismantled until it became a pile of scrap. Its Rolls-Royce Tyne turbines were used to keep the Canadair CL-44-6 Yukon in flight, registration LV-JZR of Aerotransportes Entre Ríos, which was sold on 1 November 1982 to the company Vic Air Cargo, based in the Republic Democratic Congo, where 9Q-CKQ was registered. Two years later, in 1984, the Boeing 707 registered LV-MSG Gloria was deprogrammed and cannibalised to support its twin, the LV-MZE San Jorge, which operated intermittently from Ezeiza until it was confiscated in Miami at mid-1988. By then, TAR was in an unsustainable economic situation, for which reason on 24 March 1989, it requested bankruptcy from its creditors, who filed for bankruptcy in 1990. The judicial process for the liquidation of assets of TAR took practically 13 years, concluding at the end of 2003.[38, 39]

The last remains of the Boeing 707 Gloria were scrapped at Ezeiza International Airport in 2012. The episode closed the circle that had opened at that same airport 50 years earlier in 1962, when Edgardo Luzzi dreamed of creating his own cargo company from the recovery of an interdicted plane in another bankruptcy, that of Transcontinental. Thus, with a bankruptcy at the beginning and another at the end, the history of the great Argentine freighters ended in the same place after a hyperbola of half a century, a period in which the planes of Aerotransportes Entre Ríos and TAR crossed the skies of the world, carried cargo to the farthest reaches of the planet, contributed to the prosperity of the country and in the process, made legends of all its protagonists.

BIBLIOGRAPHY

Bellini, Oscar. *Alas del Sur*. Editorial La Stampa, Buenos Aires, Argentina, 2010.

Black, Ian. Morris, Benny. *Israel's Secret Wars: A History of Israel's Intelligence Services*. Grove Press, New York, United States of America, 1991.

Drape, Michael I. *Shadows: Airlift and Airwar in biafra and Nigeria 1967–1970*. Hikoki Publications, United Kingdom, 2000.

Porter, Malcolm. *Swingtail. The Canadair CL-44 Story*. Air Britain (Historians) Ltd. United Kingdom of Great Britain and Northern Ireland, 2004

Potenze, Pablo. *Aviación Comercial Argentina, 1945–1980*. Ediciones El Cronista Comercial, Buenos Aires, 1987.

Potter, Lawrence G.; Sick, Gary. *Iran, Iraq and the Legacies of War*. Basingstoke: Palgrave Macmillan, United Kingdom, *2006*.

Rajaee, Farhang. *Iranian Perspectives on the Iran–Iraq War*. University Press of Florida, Gainesville, United States of America, 1997.

Tart, Larry. *The Price of Vigilance: Attacks on American Surveillance Flights*. Random House Publishing Group, New York, United States of America, 2001.

Timmerman, Kenneth R. *Fanning the Flames: Guns, Greed & Geopolitics in the Gulf War. The Iran Brief, Policy, Trade & Strategic Affairs*. http://www.iran.org/tib/krt/fanning_ch5.htm. Retrieved 26 January 2015.

NOTES

1 Potenze, Pablo. *Aviación Comercial Argentina, 1945–1980*. Ediciones El Cronista Comercial, Buenos Aires, 1987; p.177 and p.244.
2 Magnusson, Michael. *El Curtiss Wright C-46 en Argentina. Lima Victor*, No. 39 (Spring 2012), La Cumbre, Córdoba, Argentina, 2012; p.38.
3 Fuerza Aérea Argentina, Dirección Nacional de Transporte Aero Comercial, File N° 3411/62.
4 *Figley, Dorothy D, vs. Arrow Airlines*. Civ. N° 8128. Court of Appeal of California, Third Apellate District. 111 Cal. App. 2d 285; 244 P.2d 472; 1951 Cal. App. Lexis 1649. California, United States of America, 23 May 1952. http://www.check-six.com/Rulings/Benicia_DC-3-CoA_Opinion.htm. Retrieved 12 January 2019.
5 Public document N° 1791 dated at Buenos Aires 13 August 1969 by the Public Notary Orlando E. Bravo. Boletín Oficial de la República Argentina, Buenos Aires, Argentina, 17 September 1969.
6 Raczynski, Esteban. *Los clásicos en los Cielos del Cono Sur. Segunda parte: Argentina & Uruguay*. Ediciones SCAN, Buenos Aires, Argentina, 2005; pp.16–28.
7 Newspaper *La Capital*, Rosario, Argentina, 22 July 1972. The missing crew members in the LV-JYR were made up of the pilot Alfredo Sosa, the co-pilot Jorge Raúl Muñoz, the mechanic José María Salinas and the flight attendants Andrés Ponti, Rodolfo Jaureche and Francisco Bentancourt. Among the six dead from LV-JSY were Captain Pedro José Guerra, First Officer Richard Hofmann, and Flight Engineer Carlos DaCruz.

Chapter 2

1 Franco, Horacio. *Carlos Martínez Guerrero. Su fallecimiento*. Revista *Aeromarket*, Buenos Aires, Argentina, agosto de 1993; p.14.
2 Bellini, Oscar. *Alas del Sur*. Editorial La Stampa, Buenos Aires, Argentina, 2010; p.95–99.
3 Inspección General de Justicia. File N° 36.679 y correlative N° 258.613 of Transporte Aéreo Rioplatense S.A.
4 Miranda, Marcelo W. Historical File of Transporte Aéreo Rioplatense. Rosario, 1969–1988. Author´s archive.
5 Rodríguez Jurado, Agustín. *Curriculum vitae*. Fundación Konex, Buenos Aires, 1996. https://www.fundacionkonex.org/b1972-agustin-rodriguez-jurado. Retrieved 30 July 2018.
6 *Lease-Purchase Agreement between Airlift International Incorporated and Transporte Aéreo Rioplatense S.A*. Miami, Florida, United States; 22 January 1971. Ammendment 1, Miami, Florida, 22 January 1971. Ammendment 2, Miami, Florida, 11 March 1971.
7 United States Department of Trasportation. Federal Aviation Administration. International Field Office, United States Embassy, Buenos Aires, Argentina. Note dated 22 March 1971 to Departamento Aeronaves y Técnica of the Comando de Regiones Aéreas of the Fuerza Aérea Argentina.
8 Roberto Gaineddu. http://loudandclearisnotenought.blogspot.com.ar/2010/06/lv-jtn-canadair-cl-44d4-6-cn-34.html. Retrieved 30 March 2015.
9 Porter, Malcolm. *Swingtail. The Canadair CL-44 Story*. Air Britain (Historians) Ltd. United Kingdom of Great Britain and Northern Ireland, 2004; p.234.
10 Conti, Raúl. Notes delivered to the author, related to the accident of the Canadair CL-44 registration LV-JTN. Buenos Aires, Argentina, 9 April 2019.
11 Raczynski, Esteban. *Los clásicos en los Cielos del Cono Sur. Segunda parte: Argentina & Uruguay*. Ediciones SCAN, Buenos Aires, Argentina, 2005; p.16, p.28.
12 Van Leeuwen-Casell, Peter. *The Canadair CL-44 Archives & Preservation Trust*. http://www.cl44.com/cl44/operators.htm. Retrieved 3 August 2018.
13 Potenze, Pablo. *Aviación Comercial Argentina, 1945–1980*. Ediciones El Cronista Comercial, Buenos Aires, 1987; pp.245–246, pp.325–326.
14 Conti, Raúl. Interview with the author. Buenos Aires, Argentina, 9 April 2019.
15 Mousten, Pablo. Interview with the author. Buenos Aires, Argentina, 9 April 2019.
16 *World Airline Directory. Flight International*, 22 April 1978, p.1202.

Chapter 3

1 Magnusson, Michael. Latin glory: airlines of Latin America. Zenith Imprint, United States of America, 1995; p.12.
2 Miranda, Marcelo W. Folder of notes corresponding to the company Aerotransportes Entre Ríos. Rosario, Santa Fe, República Argentina, 1962–1970. Unpublished.
3 The crew of that first flight in 1975 to Tehran was made up of Raúl Conti (Commander), Roberto Arriague (First Officer), a co-pilot named Altamura, a Flight Engineer whose name could not be remembered, and loadmaster Oscar Palacio.
4 Confidential memorandum for information of the Chief-of-Staff of the Argentine Air Force, produced by the National Director of Commercial Air Transport. Buenos Aires, 30 July, 1981. Open Archives, H1-02-02-07-00-01-002-001-CC. Consulted in Buenos Aires, Argentina, on 15 August 2017. Unpublished.
5 Mas Godayol, José (Director). *Enciclopedia Ilustrada de la Aviación, Fascículo 146. Fuerzas Aéreas del Mundo, Irán*. Editorial Delta S.A., Barcelona, Spain, 1984.
6 Rajaee, Farhang. *Iranian Perspectives on the Iran–Iraq War*. University Press of Florida, Gainesville, United States of America, 1997.
7 Timmerman, Kenneth R. *Fanning the Flames: Guns, Greed & Geopolitics in the Gulf War. The Iran Brief, Policy, Trade & Strategic Affairs*. http://www.iran.org/tib/krt/fanning_ch5.htm. Retrieved 26 January 2015.
8 Potter, Lawrence G.; Sick, Gary. *Iran, Iraq and the Legacies of War*. Basingstoke: Palgrave Macmillan, United Kingdom, *2006*.
9 Mas Godayol, José (Director). *Enciclopedia Ilustrada de la Aviación, Fascículo 26. El Golfo Pérsico*. Editorial Delta S.A., Barcelona, Spain, 1984; p.501, p.505.

Chapter 4

1 Webman, Esther. *The challenge of assessing Arab/Islamic Atnisemitism*. Published in Middle Eastern Studies, Volume 44, Issue 5, 6 September 2010. https://www.tandfonline.com/doi/abs/10.1080/00263200903529053?journalCode=fmes20. Consulted on 14 July 2018.
2 Litvak, Meir. T*he Islamic Republic of Iran and the Holocaust: Anti-Semitism and Anti-Zionism*. Published in Journal of Israeli History, Volume 26, Issue 1, 2006. https://www.tandfonline.com/doi/abs/10.1080/13531040500502874?src=recsys&journalCode=fjih20. Consulted on 14 July 2018.
3 Brodsky, Jason M. *Israel's ties with pre-revolutionary Iran provided a road map for the Abraham Accords*. Middle East Institutute, 7 June 2023. *Iranian American Jewish Federation of New York and the Nazee & Joseph Moinian Foundation*. https://www.mei.edu/publications/israels-ties-pre-revolutionary-iran-provided-road-map-abraham-accords. Retrieved 26 August 2023.
4 Mas Godayol, José (Director). *Enciclopedia Ilustrada de la Aviación, Tomo 5. Fuerzas Aéreas del Mundo, Israel*. Editorial Delta S.A., Barcelona, Spain, 1984.
5 *Paper says Iran cheated in Weapon Deal*. Palm Beach Post, 29 April 1982 issue, p.A16. Consulted on 15 July 2018.
6 Bergman, Ronen. *The Secret War with Iran: The 30-Year Clandestine Struggle Against the World´s Most Dangerous Terrorist Power*. Simon and Schuster, New York, United States of America (9 September 2008). Consulted 22 July 2018.
7 Thomas Gordon. *Gideon's Spies: The Secret History of the Mossad*. St. Martin's Press, New York, United States of America, 1999.
8 Black, Ian. Morris, Benny. *Israel's Secret Wars: A History of Israel's Intelligence Services*. Grove Press, New York, United States of America, 1991.
9 Perlmutter, Amos; Michael I. Handel y Bar-Joseph Uri. *Two Minutes over Baghdad*. Frank Cass Publishers; London, Great Britain, 2008; p. 40. ISBN 978-0-7146-8347-8.
10 Simons, Geoff. *Iraq: From Sumer to Saddam*. Palgrave Macmillan, 2004; p.320. ISBN 978-1403917706.
11 Solis, Gary D. *The Law of Armed Conflict: International Humanitarian Law in War*. Cambridge University Press, Great Britain, 2010; p.182. ISBN 978-0521870887.

12 Dan Reiter. Preventive Attacks against Nuclear Programs and the "Success" at Osiraq. *Nonproliferation Review.*, Vol. 12, No 2, July 2005. The Monterey Institute of International Studies, Centre for Nonproliferation Studies, United States of America, 2005.

13 Schneider, Barry R. Radical Responses to Radical Regimes: Evaluating Preemptive Counter-Proliferation, May 1995. Institute for National Strategic Studies. National Defence University. McNair Paper, Fort McNair, Washington, May 1995, p.41,

14 http://www.f-16.net/f-16_users_article7.html

15 Dupuy, Trevor; Paul Martell. *Flawed Victory: Arab-Israeli Conflict and the 1982 War in Lebanon.* Hero Books, United States of America, 1986; p.69. ISBN 978-0915979073.

16 Lewin, Avraham Shmuel. Osirak Revisited. Published in FrontPage Magazine. The Jewish Press. Tuesday, 18 December 2007. http://archive.frontpagemag.com/readArticle.aspx?ARTID=29258. Consulted on 30 December 2014.

17 Seale, Patrick. *Asad: The Struggle for the Middle East.* University of California Press, United States of America, 1990; p.370. ISBN 978-0520069763.

18 Raas, Whitney; Austin Long. *Osirak Redux? Assessing Israeli Capabilities to Destroy Iranian Nuclear Facilities.* Published in International Security (Belfer Center for Science and International Affairs), Volume 31, issue 4, Spring 2007; p.7 [33] http://belfercenter.ksg.harvard.edu/publication/850/osirak_redux_assessing_israeli_capabilities_to_destroy_iranian_nuclear_facilities.html. Consulted 30 December 2014.

Chapter 5

1 United States of America. Congress House. Committee on Foreign Affairs. Task Force to Investigate Certain Allegations Concerning the Holding of American Hostages by Iran in 1980. Joint report of the Task Force to Investigate Certain Allegations Concerning the Holding of American Hostages by Iran in 1980 ("October Surprise Task Force"). United States of America, 1993, p.166.

2 Sick, Gary. October Surprise: America´s hostages in Iran and the election of Ronald Reagan. Times Books, New York, 1991; p.111, p.278.

3 Broug, Alan. Tango Romeo – The life and times of Jack Malloch. www.jackmalloch.com. Retrieved 15 July 2014.

4 Aero Transport Data Bank. http://www.aerotransport.org/php/go.php?query=operator&where=56950&luck. Retrieved 13 February 2015.

5 Seagrave, Sterling. Un caballero errante del aire. Grandes Epocas de la Aviación, Tomo N° 16 (Soldados de Fortuna II). Ediciones Folio SA, Barcelona, Spain, 1995; p.124.

6 Broug, Alan. Email addressed to Gustavo Marón on 28 September 2014. Author's archive.

7 Ibid, on 23 October 2014. Author's file.

8 Drape, Michael I. Shadows: Airlift and Airwar in biafra and Nigeria 1967–1970. Hikoki Publications, United Kingdom, 2000; p.63, p.121.

9 http://www.airliners.net/aviation-forums/general_aviation/print.main?id=2644486. Retrieved 12 March 2015.

10 http://www.aerobernie.bplaced.net/Affretair.html. Retrieved 12 March 2015.

11 Broug, Alan. Email addressed to Gustavo Marón on 25 September 2014 at 0:51. Author's file.

12 Nesbit, Roy y Dudley Cowderoy. Sanctions busters. FLIGHT International, 2 February 1985; pp.26–27.

13 Biography´s Jack Malloch. In Soldiers of Fortune, Mercenary Wars. 2010. http://www.mercenary-wars.net/biography/jack-malloch.html. Retrieved 14 March 2015.

14 http://www.planespotters.net/Airline/CargOman

15 FLIGHT International, 2 June 1979, p.1894.

16 FitzGerald, Cecilia Elisei & Agustina Saubidet. Rumbo y Fe. Miguel L. FitzGerald. Editorial Lápiz en Mano, Buenos Aires, Argentina, 2012; p.129, p.157.

17 Transporte Aéreo Rioplatense SA. Note addressed by Engineer Federico N. Gioja, Technical Manager of the company, to the Aircraft Inspector Jacinto Antonio González. Buenos Aires, Argentina, 7 July, 1981. Unpublished.

18 Seoane, María y Vicente Muleiro. El dictador. La historia secreta y pública de Jorge Rafael Videla. Editorial Sudamericana, Buenos Aires, Argentina, 2001; p.307.

19 Diario O Comunista, N° 44, segunda serie. *São Paulo, Brasil,* 25 July 1977. https://1969revolucaoressaca.blogspot.com/2017/07/1977-07-25-o-comunista-n-44-ii-serie.html. Retrieved 25 July 2018.

20 Arandar, Eduardo. Odisea en el Caribe de un avión argentino. La Semana, Buenos Aires, Argetnina, 6 July 1977.

21 According to emails sent by Héctor Biondini to the author on 14 and 16 February 2019, the weapons seized in Barbados had been purchased in Great Britain from the Czechoslovak distributor OMNIPOL, which dispatched them to Lisbon to be shipped there on the CL-44 of TAR. 'Since the autonomy of the plane did not allow us to reach Guatemala, the genius who designed the navigation did not come up with a better idea than to make a technical stopover in Barbados, a former English colony, when the Fort Lauderdale international airport was almost the same distance away, de-France (in French Martinique), where the arrival of the plane would not cause problems. MI5 or MI6 was trying to stop the plane at any cost, because Guatemala was threatening to invade the British colony of Belize, and TAR delivered it to them on a platter. It was one more Argentine bungling, born of ignorance, of not knowing political geography. They landed there as a technical stopover and they all immediately ended up in jail, with the plane and weapons seized by the authorities. TAR, in this type of operations, was advised by Maxwell Smart, Super Agent 86'.

Chapter 6

1 República Argentina. Ministry of Defence. Open Files. Original contract in English on four pages and translation into Spanish on five pages entered into between Transportes Aéreos Rioplatenses and Stuart J. McCafferty. Position H1-020-02-07-00-01-0001-001-CC. Consulted in Buenos Aires, National Library of Aeronautics, on 15 July 2016.

2 Joseph, Gilbert M. y Daniela Spenser. *In from the Cold: Latin America´s new encounter with the Cold War.* Duke University Press Books, United States, 2008; p.165.

3 Spenser, Daniela. *Espejos de la Guerra Fría: México, América Central y el Caribe.* Centro de Investigaciones y Estudios Superiores en Antropología Social, Mexico, 2004; p.335.

4 Fuerza Aérea Argentina. Comando de Regiones Aéreas. Junta de Investigaciones de Accidentes de Aviación. File N° C.E. 998.720 (FAA). Disposición N° 102/81. Buenos Aires, Argentina, 10 September 1981. Unpublished.

5 Sopeña, Germán & Mario Diament. *A las armas las carga el diablo... pero las trafican los hombres.* Revista *Siete Días*, Año XIV, N° 737 (29 July – 4 August 1981). Editorial CREA SA, Buenos Aires, República Argentina, 1981; p.4, p.11.

6 Héctor Biondini. Email addressed to the author. Buenos Aires, Argentina, 8 February 2019.

7 Melo, Roberto. Chats addressed to the author, Buenos Aires, Argentina, 10 and 11 April 2019.

8 International Criminal Police Organisation (INTERPOL). *What is INTERPOL?* https://www.interpol.int/ipsgapp/educational/what-is-interpol.html. Retrieved 5 August 2018.

9 Broug, Alan. Email addressed to Gustavo Marón on 28 September 2014.

10 International Air Transport Association. *Airline and Airport code.* https://www.iata.org/publications/Pages/code-search.aspx. Retrieved 16 February 2019.

11 Palacio, Oscar. Interview with the author. Buenos Aires, Argentina, 26 March 2015.

12 Bergman, Ronen. *The secret war with Iran: The 30-year clandestine struggle against the world´s most dangeorus terrorist power.* Free Press, United States, 2008; pp.41– 47.

13 Porter, Malcolm. *Swingtail. The Canadair CL-44 Story.* Air Britain-Historians Limited, United Kingdom of Great Britain, 2004; p.136.

14 *1981–1983: US Launches Military PSYOPS Missions Designed to Agitate, Frighten Soviets.* History Commons. http://www.historycommons.org/context.jsp?item=a19811983ussrpsyops. Retrieved 30 January 2015.

15 Schaefer, Bernd, Nate Jones & Benjamin B. Fischer. *Forecasting Nuclear War: Stasi/KGB Intelligence Cooperation Under Project RYAN.* Published 13 November 2014. https://www.wilsoncenter.org/publication/forecasting-nuclear-war. Retrieved 5 August 2018.

16 *"Flying outside ATS routes prohibited"*. Atlas 20H.L, Near East, 16 November 1989 issue. Atlas 15H.L SW USSR, 21 September 1989 issue.
17 It was precisely in an El Al Israel Bristol Britannia that Israeli commandos transferred Nazi war criminal Adolf Eichman from Ezeiza to Tel Aviv, whom they had previously kidnapped in Buenos Aires in May 1960.
18 Sopeña, Germán & Mario Diament. *A las armas las carga el diablo… pero las trafican los hombres*. Revista *Siete Días*, Año XIV, N° 737 (29 July – 4 August 1981). Editorial CREA SA, Buenos Aires, República Argentina, 1981; p.4, p.11.

Chapter 7

1 Syrtlanov, Marat. *November tango*. Published in Rossia, Moscow, Russian Federation, 7 June 2007. Translation from Russian to Spanish by Miguel Borisov. Mendoza, 22 December 2014. http://nvo.ng.ru/realty/2015-12-25/1_tango.html. Accessed 12 December 2014.
2 *Recconaissance flight over the USSR*. Updated 30 January 2004. Giebelstadt Air Base Home Pay http://www.c-and-e-museum.org/Pinetreeline/giebelstadt/gieb-other/other/ogieb-8.html. Accessed 15 August 2018. http://www.pinetreeline.org/giebelstadt/gieb-other/other/ogieb-8.html. The espionage Canberra was in 540 RAF Squadron and was probably registered WH726.
3 Lednicer, David. *Aircraft Downed During the Cold War and Thereafter*. Last revised: 8 November 2005. http://sw.propwashgang.org/shootdown_list.html. Accessed 15 August 2018. The C-118 (registration 51-3822, construction number 43569/253) was the personal aircraft of Allen Dulles, then Director of the CIA. The flight started in Wiesbaden (West Germany) and had Karachi (Pakistan) as its final destination. It was reported that on the leg between Cyprus and Iran the plane was carrying 'highly sensitive military technology'. The Russian pilots who scored the kill were G.F. Svetlichnikov and B.F. Zakharov. The five passengers on board saved their lives by parachuting while the four crew members survived the emergency landing.
4 http://aviation-safety.net/database/record.php?id=19580627-1&lang=es. Crewmen Dale D. Brannon, Luther W. Lyles, Robert E. Crans, Bennie A. Shupe, James T. Kane, James N. Luther, James G. Holman, Earl H. Reamer, and Peter N. Sabo were captured and later liberated by the Soviets on 7 July 1958.
5 Lednicer, David. *Intrusions, Overflights, Shootdowns and Defections During the Cold War and Thereafter.* Last revised: 26 December 2017. http://myplace.frontier.com/~anneled/ColdWar.html. Consulted on 15 August 2018.
6 *Criminal Occurrence despription*. https://aviation-safety.net/database/record.php?id=19610804-0. Accessed 15 August 2018. The aircraft carried the Iranian civilian registration EP-ADK.
7 Mladenov, Alexander. *Soviet Cold War Fighters*. Fonthill Media Limited, United States of America, 2016.
8 American Cold War Veterans. http://www.americancoldwarvets.org/cold-war-casualties.
9 *Wings Palette*. http://wp.scn.ru/en/forum/in_focus/13-1-10. Accessed 15 March 2015. The pilot of the MiG-19 was V. P. Pavlovskii. The pilot of the MiG-17 was Pechenkin. Both were in the 156th Fighter Aviation Regiment-
10 Lednicer, David. *Aircraft downed during the Cold War and thereafter*. Last revised 8 November 2005. http://sw.propwashgang.org/shootdown_list.html. Accessed 14 August 2018.
11 Wise, James E. (Jr) & Scott Baron. *Dangerous Games. Faces, incidents and casualties of the Cold War*. Naval Institute Press, Annapolis, Maryland, United States of America, 2010.
12 Samuel, Wolfgang W.E. *I Always Wanted to Fly: America's Cold War Airmen*. Jackson University Press of Mississippi, United States of America, 2001; p.151.
13 http://www.pacificaviationmuseum.org/pearl-harbor-blog/north-american-f-100f-super-sabre-s-n-58-1232
14 'Soviet Downs Iranian Helicopter After It Strays, Killing the Crew'. *The New York Times newspaper,* 18 July edition. https://www.nytimes.com/1978/07/18/archives/soviet-downs-iranian-helicopter-after-it-strays-killing-the-crew.html. Retrieved 16 August 2018. The pilot of the first MiG-23M was A.V. Dem'janov, the author of the demolitions was V.I. Shkinder. Shortly after the episode, the Soviets allowed the damaged helicopter to be repaired by the Iranians, authorising the return to Iran with its crew shortly after.
15 Safarik, Jan Josef. *Air to Air Victories of SSSR during Cold War*. http://aces.safarikovi.org/
16 Cooper, Tom. *Project Dark Gene and Project IBEX*. www.acig.org. Posted 15 February 2009. Accessed 30 January 2019. Also http://www.spyflight.co.uk/darkgene.htm. Consulted on 30 January 2019.
17 Mas Godayol, José (Director). *Enciclopedia Ilustrada de la Aviación, Fascículo 136. Fuerzas Aéreas del Mundo, Turquía*. Editorial Delta S.A., Barcelona, Spain, 1984.
18 Mas Godayol, José (Director). *Enciclopedia Ilustrada de la Aviación, Fascículo 101. El flanco sur de la OTAN*. Editorial Delta S.A., Barcelona, Spain, 1984; pp.2001–2004.
19 http://www.globalsecurity.org/space/facility/pirinclik.htm
20 Siebert, W.M. *The early history of pulse compression radar – The development of AN/FPS-17 coded-pulse radar at Lincoln Laboratory*. IEEE Transactions on Aerospace and Electronic Systems, Volume 24, Issue 6, Nov 1988. Adelphi, Maryland, United States of America, pp.833–837.
21 Delaney William P. & William W. Ward. *Radar Development at Lincoln Laboratory: An Overview of the First Fifty Years.* Publicado en *Lincoln Laboratory Journal*, Volume 12, Number 2. Cambridge, Massachusetts, United States of America.2000, pp.147–166.
22 United States of America. Central Intelligence Agency. *Air Defence of the USSR. Interagency Intelligence Memorandum Summary.* Document 307875 1-86. Originally classified as ultra secret (Top Secret). Declassified and sanitised (Release as sanitised) in October 1999 within the framework of the CIA Historical Review Program. https://www.cia.gov/library/readingroom/docs/DOC_0000261292.pdf. Accessed 5 January 2019.
23 United States of America. Central Intelligence Agency. *The Readiness of Soviet Air Forces.* Interagency Intelligence Memorandum Summary. Document NI II 82-1001 JX. Originally classified as ultra secret (Top Secret). April 1982. Declassified and sanitised (Release as sanitised) in October 1999 within the framework of the CIA Historical Review Program. https://www.cia.gov/library/readingroom/docs/DOC_0000261313.pdf. Accessed 5 January 2019.
24 Bishop, Farzad & Tom Cooper. *Iranian F-4 Phantom II units in combat.* Osprey Combat Aicraft N° 37. Osprey Publishing Limited, Great Britain, 2003.
25 Cooper, Tom and Farzad Bishop. *Target: Saddam´s Reactor. Israeli and Iranian operations against Iraqi plans to develop nuclear weapons.* http://www.angelfire.com/art2/narod/opera/ Accessed 26 December 2014.
26 Syrtlanov, Marat. *Feat under seven presses.* http://www.psj.ru/saver_magazins/detail.php?ID=2561. Consulted on 10 April 2015. Published in Russia, 28 June 2006. Translation from Russian to Spanish by Miguel Borisov. Mendoza, 24 April 2015.
27 Kulyapin, Valentin. Interview conducted at the RosCosmos Television Studio, Moscow, Russia, in September 2010. http://sandar.ucoz.ru/forum/7-38-1. Accessed 10 February 2015. Public translation by Miguel Borisov. Mendoza, 1 April 2015.

Chapter 8

1 Peter Danssaert & Sergio Finardi. *The Arms Flyers. Commercial Aviation, Human Rights, and the Business of War and Arms.* Antwerp and Chicago, June 2011. *International Peace Information Service* (IPIS). Retrieved 5 August 2018.
2 Yasmann, Víctor J. *The KGB documents and the Soviet collpase.* National Council for Eurasian and East European Research, London, United Kingdom of Great Britain and Northern Ireland, 1998.
3 Ben-Menashe, Ari. *Profits of War: Inside the secret US – Israeli Arms Network*. Sheridan Square Press, New York, United States of America, 1992; Chapter 7.
4 United States Department of Defense. *Dictionary of Military and associates terms.* Joint Publication 1-02. Washington, DC, United States of America, 12 April 2001. https://web.archive.org/web/20091108082044/http://www.dtic.mil/doctrine/jel/new_pubs/jp1_02.pdf. Retrieved 11 September 2018.
5 United States of America, Department of the Air Force. *Operations. Reporting meaconing, intrussion, jamming and interference of electromagnetic systems.* Washington,

DC, United States of America, 31 July 1986. https://www.marines.mil/Portals/59/Publications/MCO%203430.3C.pdf?ver=2012-10-11-163623-383. Retrieved 11 September 2018.

6 United States of America. Department of the Army, Headquarters. *Communications Techniques: Electronic Counter-Conutermeasures.* Washington, DC, United States of America, 17 July 1990. https://fas.org/irp/doddir/army/fm24-33/fm243_5.htm. Retrieved 11 September 2018.

7 United States of America. Department of the Navy. *Navy Information Systems Technician Training Series.* Module 1. http://informationtechniciantraining.tpub.com/14222/css/Meaconing-Intrusion-Jamming-And-Interference-Miji-88.htm. Retrieved 11 September 2018.

8 Kuzichkin, Vladimir. *Inside the KGB. Phanteon*, New York, United States of America, 1991.

9 Tart, Larry. *The Price of Vigilance: Attacks on American Surveillance Flights.* Random House Publishing Group, New York, United States of America, 2001.

10 Willingham, Charles. *In My Time: The Greatest Century of Change in the History of Man.* iUniverse, Lincoln, Nebraska, United States of America, 2007.

11 *List of tallest structures built in the Soviet Union.* https://en.wikipedia.org/wiki/List_of_tallest_structures_built_in_the_Soviet_Union. Retrieved 11 September 2018.

12 http://www.radiojamming.puslapiai.lt/photo.htm. Retrieved 11 September 2018.

13 Syrtlanov, Marat. *"Accidental" collision.* http://www.trud.ru/article/24-08-2001/28881_sluchajnoe_stolknovenie.html www.trud.ru/article/24-08-2001/28881_sluchajnoe_stolknovenie.html. Consulted on 20 October 2014. Translation from Russian to Spanish by Miguel Borisov in Mendoza, Argentina, on 5 November 2014.

14 41° 37' 42" North Latitude – 45° 01' 59" East Longitude.

15 http://www.ww2.dk/new/air%20force/regiment/iap/982iap.htm. Retrieved 11 September 2011.

16 40° 08′50′′ North Latitude, 44° 23′ 45′′ East Longitude.

17 Vasquez, Tim. *Soviet & Russian Airfields Master List.* Uptated 8 Sep 09. www.weathergraphics.com/tim/russia/sovietbase.xls. Retrieved 25 January 2015.

18 10:18 a.m. Ankara time, 4:18 p.m. Coordinated Universal Time (UTC).

19 Ordinary telegram received No. 56,836, Cable No. 337 issued on 16 September 1981 by Ambassador Rodolfo Etchegoyen (Ankara). File of the Ministry of Foreign Affairs and Worship, Section 71 (Communications), Turkey, Cables received Ankara, 1981, Box No. AH/0295. S. Topographic: C.71 A.118.

20 Grebneva, Natalia. *5 самых известных случаев вторжения в воздушное пространство СССР ИНЦИДЕНТ CL-44.* ("Five Most Famous Cases of the Invasion of Soviet Airspace. CL-44 Incident"). http://smartnews.ru/articles/10455.html#ixzz3CkpheNDe. Accessed 25 January 2015.

21 Горячее небо «холодной войны». Часть 3. // Мир авиации : журнал. (Hot sky "cold war". Part 3 // magazine World aviation. – Moscow, Russia,1996. – № 2 (12). – S. 38-42. http://www.airforce.ru/awm/ hotsky/hotsky3.htm Accessed 12 September 2018.

22 http://oper.ru/oforum/read.php?thread_id=1049505764&page=4. Retrieved 14 September 2018.

23 Инциденты "Холодной войны". ("Cold War" incidents). http://www.skywar.ru/389.html. Accessed 25 January 2015.

24 Annex 2 (Rules of the Air) of the International Civil Aviation Agreement signed in 1944 in Chicago. Sixth Edition, approved 25 May 1970, effective 25 September 1970, and applicable 4 February 1971. Catalogue of ICAO Publications, Montreal, Canada, 1981. https://www.icao.int/ Meetings/anconf12/Document%20Archive/an02_cons%5B1%5D.pdf. Accessed September 14, 2018.

25 Butowski, P. *Sukhoi Su-15 'Flagon'. Technical Specifications Su-15 Family*, publicado en *International Air Power Review* volume 1, David Donald editor, AIRtime Publishing, United States of America, 2001. Cited in *Milavia.* https://www.milavia.net/aircraft/su-15/su-15_specifications.htm. Retrieved 15 September 2018.

26 Canadair. *CL-44D-4 Flying Operating Manual.* Cartierville, Canada, 1964.

27 Burbyga, N. The little-known collision of Captain Kulyapin. News Magazine, Moscow, Russian Federation, 1991. Translation by Miguel Borisov, Mendoza, Argentina, 30 September 2014.

28 Singfield, Tom. *Classic Airliners. 76 older types, worldwide, described and illustrated in colour.* Midland Publishing, England, pp.56, 57, 108–109.

29 Mas Godayol, José (Director). *Enciclopedia Ilustrada de la Aviación, Fascículo 27. Líneas Aéreas del mundo, Aeroflot.* Editorial Delta S.A., Barcelona, Spain, 1984.

30 Yaroshevskii, Anatoly. *100 лет полет нормальный.* (100 years of normal flight). Первый канал, First Channel, 2012. http://www.1tv.ru/documentary/print/fi=7700. Accessed 10 February 2014.

31 *ВТОРОЙ В МИРЕ ТАРАН НА РЕАКТИВНОМ САМОЛЕТЕ.* (The second taran in the world in a jet plane). Segodnya newspaper, issue No. 1395 of 4 March 2003. http://www.segodnya.ua/oldarchive/c2256713004f33f5c2256cde003c1491.html. Accessed 24 March 2015.

32 Syrtlanov, Marat. Feat under seven presses. http://www.psj.ru/saver_magazins/detail.php?ID=2561. Consulted on 10 April 2015. Published in Russia, 28 June 2006. Translation from Russian to Spanish by Miguel Borisov. Mendoza, 24 April 2015.

33 Syrtlanov, Marat. *"Accidental" collision.* Published in Trud, Moscow, Russian Federation, on 24 August 2001. Translation from Russian to Spanish by Miguel Borisov. Mendoza, Argentina, 5 November 2014. http://www.trud.ru/article/24-08-2001/28881_sluchajnoe_stolknovenie.html www.trud.ru/article/24-08-2001/28881_sluchajnoe_stolknovenie.html. Accessed 1 November 2014.

34 *ВТОРОЙ В МИРЕ ТАРАН НА РЕАКТИВНОМ САМОЛЕТЕ.* (The second taran in the world in a jet plane). Segodnya newspaper, issue No. 1395 of 4 March 2003. http://www.segodnya.ua/oldarchive/c2256713004f33f5c2256cde003c1491.html. Accessed 24 March 2015.

35 Fedorov, Vyacheslav. *ПРИКАЗАНО — СБИТЬ. Ordered Downed. Part IV.*
Again the old. http://knu.znate.ru/docs/index-462107.html y www.chvvaul.net. Retrieved 10 February 2015.

36 http://www.airaces.narod.ru/all9/kulypin2.jpg. Retrieved 30 March 2015.

37 Kuchin, Vladimir y Nishny Novgorod. семирная волновая история (World Wave of History). Moscow, 2013. http://alpan365.ru/vsemirnaya-volnovaya-istoriya/v-kuchin-vsemirnaya-volnovaya-istoriya-1980-1984-gg/. Accessed 24 March 2015.

38 Kulyapin, Valentin. Interview conducted at the RosCosmos Television Studio, Moscow, Russia, in September 2010. http://sandar.ucoz.ru/forum/7-38-1. Accessed 10 February 2015. Public translation by Miguel Borisov. Mendoza, 1 April 2015.

39 Fedorov, Vyacheslav. *ПРИКАЗАНО — СБИТЬ. Ordered Downed. Part IV.*
Again the old. http://knu.znate.ru/docs/index-462107.html y www.chvvaul.net. Retrieved 10 February 2015.

40 Kanevsky, Anatoly. *Таран – это по-нашему* (*Tarán is our way*). АВИАПАНОРАМА Magazine (Aviapanorama) No. 56, 13 April 2006. «Высокие технологии и инновации» (High Technologies and Innovations, Ltd). Moscow, Russian Federation, 2006. http://aviapanorama.su/2006/04/taran-eto-po-nashemu/. Accessed 21 March 2015.

41 Secret telegram received No. 47,845, Cable No. 292 –Very Urgent – issued on 28 July 1981 by Ambassador José Luis Vignolo (Ankara). File of the Ministry of Foreign Affairs and Worship, Section 71 (Communications), Turkey, Cables received Ankara, 1981, Box No. AH/0295. S. Topographic: C.71 A.118.

42 Carnero, José Edgard. *Las reglamentaciones aeronáuticas. El modelo argentino.* Serie Perspectivas. Editorial FUNDEC, Buenos Aires, Argentina. 2004, p.88, p.90.

43 FitzGerald, Cecilia Elisei & Agustina Saubidet. *Rumbo y Fe. Miguel L. FitzGerald.* Editorial Lápiz en Mano, Buenos Aires, 2012; p.129, p.157.

44 Secret telegram issued No. 35,268, Cable No. 536 –Very Urgent – issued on 1 August 1981 by the Eastern Europe Department of the Foreign Ministry, destined for the Argentine Embassy in Moscow. Archive of the Ministry of Foreign Affairs and Worship, Section 71

(Communications), USSR, Cables issued Moscow, 1981, Box No. AH/0142. S. Topographic: C.72 A.143.

45 Syrtlanov, Marat. *"Accidental" collision*. In Trud, No. 155. Moscow, Russian Federation, 24 August 2001 edition. Translation by Miguel Borisov, 5 November 2014. http://www.trud.ru/article/24-08-2001/28881_sluchajnoe_stolknovenie.html. Consulted on 28 October 2018.

Chapter 9

1 Newspaper *Los Andes*, Mendoza, Argentina, 4 August 1981, p.1.

2 Ordinary telegram issued No. 35,702, Cable No. 545 issued on 5 August 1981 by the General Directorate of Press and Diffusion of the Foreign Ministry destined for the Argentine Embassy in Moscow and Tehran. Archive of the Ministry of Foreign Affairs and Worship, Section 71 (Communications), USSR, Cables issued Moscow, 1981, Box No. AH/0142. S. Topographic: C.72 A.143.

3 Newspaper *Los Andes*, Mendoza, Argentina. 11 August 1981, p.2.

4 Kulyapin, Valentin. Interview conducted at the RosCosmos Television Studio, Moscow, Russia, in September 2010. http://sandar.ucoz.ru/forum/7-38-1. Accessed 10 February 2015. Public translation by Miguel Borisov. Mendoza, 1 April 2015.

5 Dabrowski, Krzysztof. *Cold War Taran*. Air Combat Information Group (ACIG). 17 July 2012 at 09:34 PM. http://www.acig.info/CMS/index.php?option=com_content&task=view&id=261&Itemid=47. Last revised 22 December 2012 12:49 PM. Accessed 3 April 2015.

6 Eltvik, Johan Vilhelm. Interview with Valentin Kulyapin conducted in Moscow, Russia, November 2012, published 17 November 2012 on the Young Men's Christian Association (YMCA) blog. http://thebluemusicblog.ymca.int/2012/11/17/valentins-day-1981-ussr/#comment-4804

7 Marón, Gustavo. *Juliet Tango November. Un crimen de la Guerra Fría encubierto por cinco Estados*. Editorial Grupo Abierto, Buenos Aires, Argentina, 2019.

8 Among the more than 300 people classified as 'dangerous' were the artists and writters Norma Aleandro, Emilio Alfaro, Osvaldo Bayer, Héctor Alterio, Norman Briski, Julio Cortázar, Roberto Cossa, Rogelio García Lupo, Eva Giberti, Horacio Guarany, Víctor Heredia, Cipe Lincovsky, Federico Luppi, Osvaldo Pugliese, Mercedes Sosa and María Elena Walsh.

9 *Se derrumba la sede de la Fuerza Aérea Argentina*. Newspaper *El País*, Madrid, Spain, 6 December 1980. https://elpais.com/diario/1980/12/06/internacional/344905201_850215.html. Retrieved 25 February 2019.

10 Boletín Oficial de la República Argentina, edition of 26 December 1968, Contracts Section. https://archive.org/stream/Boletin_Oficial_Republica_Argentina_2da_seccion_1968-12-26/1968-12-26_djvu.txt. Consulted on 13 November 2018.

11 Boletín Oficial de la República Argentina, edition of 30 September 1969, Contracts Section. https://archive.org/stream/Boletin_Oficial_Republica_Argentina_2da_seccion_1969-09-30/1969-09-30_djvu.txt. Consulted on 13 November 2018.

12 Boletín Oficial de la República Argentina, edition of 4 August 1977, Contracts Section. https://archive.org/stream/Boletin_Oficial_Republica_Argentina_2da_seccion_1977-08-04/1977-08-04_djvu.txt Accessed on 12 November 2018.

13 Anonymous document left under the door of all the departments of the building located at Calle Chenault No. 1968 in the Federal Capital of the Argentine Republic on 29 December 1988. Sent to Marcelo W. Miranda on 2 May 1997 at 7: 43AM by FAX 541260287. Gustavo Marón Archive. Unpublished.

14 Gilbert, Isidoro. *El oro de Moscú. Historia secreta de la diplomacia, el comercio y la inteligencia soviética en la Argentina*. Editorial Sudamericana, Buenos Aires, República Argentina, 2007; p.430.

15 Paxton, John. *The Statesman´s Year-Book 1976–1977*. Palgrave McMillan, Basignstoke, United Kingdom of Great Britain and Northern Ireland, 1977.

16 Paxton, John. *The Statesman´s Year-Book 1977–1978*. Palgrave McMillan, Basignstoke, United Kingdom of Great Britain and Northern Ireland, 1978.

17 Portugheis, Elsa. *Bombardeo del 16 de junio de 1955*. Unidad Especial de Investigación sobre Terrorismo de Estado delArchivo Nacional de la Memoria. Ministerio de Justicia, Seguridad y Derechos Humanos de la Nación. Buenos Aires, 2010. http://www.hcdavellaneda.gob.ar/upload/images/1434408266Bombardeo%20Plaza%20de%20Mayo%201955.pdf. Retrieved 14 November 2018.

18 Canelo, Paula. *La descomposición del poder militar en la Argentina. Las Fuerzas Armadas durante las presidencias de Galtieri, Bignone y Alfonsín (1981–1987)*. Programa Interuniversitario de Historia Política. http://historiapolitica.com/datos/biblioteca/ochentas_canelo.pdf. Retrieved 14 November 2018.

19 http://www.telam.com.ar/notas/201702/178682-lami-dozo-absuelto-por-el-juicio-a-las-juntas-condenado-por-malvinas-e-indultado-por-menem.html. Retrieved 14 November 2018.

20 Canelo, Paula. *El gobierno del 'Proceso' en el nivel provincial. Reclutamiento, rol y carreras políticas de los interventores y gobernadores de la última dictadura militar argentina (1976–1983)*. X Jornadas de Sociología. Facultad de Ciencias Sociales, Universidad de Buenos Aires, Buenos Aires, 2013. http://www.peronlibros.com.ar/sites/default/files/pdfs/canelo-_el_gobierno_del_procesoo_en_el_nivel_provincial._reclutamiento_rol_y_carreras_politicas_de_los_interventores_y_gob.pdf. Retrieved 14 Novmeber 2018.

21 Thwaites Rey, Mabel. *Alas rotas. La política de privatización y quiebra de Aerolíneas Argentinas*. Temas Grupo Editorial SRL, Buenos Aires, República Argentina, 2001; p.54.

22 Bellini, Oscar. *Alas del Sur*. Editorial Rumbo 180, Buenos Aires, República Argentina, 2010; p.99.

23 Yofre, Juan Bautista. *1982. Los documentos secretos de la Guerra de Malvinas/Falklands y el derrumbe del Proceso*. Editorial Sudamericana, Buenos Aires, Argentina, 2011; p.65.

24 Lami Dozo, Basilio. Interview given to the newspaper Perfil, Buenos Aires, Argentina, 22 November 2009. https://www.perfil.com/noticias/elobservador/despues-de-las-islas-pensabamos-atacar-chile.phtml. Consulted on 17 November 2018.

25 The preventive deployment of British forces had begun several days earlier, on 29 March 1982, when the Joint Intelligence Committee reported that an Argentine invasion of the islands was imminent, for which Margaret Thatcher ordered the preventive displacement of three nuclear submarines to the south of the islands. The submarine HMS *Spartan* left Gibraltar on 30 April HMS *Splendid* left Faslane on 1 April and HMS *Conqueror* put to sea on 3 April, one day after the Argentine occupation of the Falklands.

26 Boletín Oficial de la República Argentina, Buenos Aires, Argentina, 21 July 1971.

27 Franco, Horacio Víctor. *Carlos Martínez Guerrero, su fallecimiento*. Aeromarket Magazine, Buenos Aires, Argentine Republic, August 1993 edition; p.14.

28 Fuerza Aérea Argentina. File N° 1.608.749.

29 Héctor Biondini. Interview with Gustavo Marón, Buenos Aires, 15 July 2015.

30 Blumenthal, Ralph. Gander crash puts spotlight on aviation group and its regulatory clashes. Published in The New York Times, 24 December 1985. https://www.nytimes.com/1985/12/24/us/gander-crash-puts-spotlight-on-aviation-group-and-its-regulatory-clashes.html. Accessed 10 January 2019.

31 Miranda, Marcelo W. File corresponding to Rioplatense Air Transport. Author's file. Consulted in Mendoza, Argentine Republic, on 18 November 2018.

32 *1982 Falklands War Timeline. A Chronology of events during the Falklands Conflict of 1982*. https://web.archive.org/web/20100327150403/http://www.falklands.info/history/82timeline.html. Retrieved 18 November 2018.

33 Martin, Lisa L. *Institutions and Cooperation: Sanctions during the Falkland Inslands Conflict*. Publicado en *International Security*, Vol. 16, No 4 (Spring 1992). The MIT Press, Cambridge, Massachusetts, United States of America. https://web.stanford.edu/class/ips216/Readings/martin_92.pdf. Consultado el 18 de noviembre de 2018.

34 República Argentina, Ministerio de Defensa. Fuerza Aérea Argentina, Note FA No. 5040039, of 22 November 1982, addressed by the Chief of General Staff of the Argentine Air Force to the Minister of Economy of the Nation. Open Files, position A1-00-

00-14-00-01-002. Consulted at the National Aeronautical Library, Buenos Aires, Argentina, on 15 August 2017. Unpublished.

35 República Argentina, Ministerio de Defensa. Fuerza Aérea Argentina. Note No. 1,608,882 of 18 November 1982 addressed by the National Director of Commercial Air Transport to Jeve V (Aeronautical Interests) of the General Staff of the Argentine Air Force. Open Files, position A1-00-00-14-00-01-004. Consulted at the National Aeronautical Library, Buenos Aires, Argentina, on 15 August 2017. Unpublished.

36 Anonymous document left under the door of all the departments of the building located at Calle Chenault No.1968 in the Federal Capital of the Argentine Republic on 29 December 1988. Sent to Marcelo W. Miranda on 2 May 1997 at 7: 43AM by FAX 541260287. Gustavo Marón Archive. Unpublished.

37 Boletín Oficial de la República Argentina. Edition of 16 May 1989. Year XCVII, number 26,634. Section Contracts of Limited Liability Companies. Entry corresponding to Aerotransportes Entre Ríos SRL.

38 Miranda, Marcelo W. Notes included in the file corresponding to Transporte Aéreo Rioplatense SA. Rosario, Santa Fe, Argentine Republic, 1990.

39 Poder Judicial de la Nación. Juzgado Nacional de Primera Instancia en lo Comercial N° 4, Secretaría N° 7, Capital Federal. Expediente "*Transporte Aéreo Rioplatense sobre quiebra*". Judicial edict informed the project of final distribution and final regulation of fees. Official Bulletin of the Argentine Republic, edition of 22 September 2003.

ABOUT THE AUTHOR

Gustavo Marón was born in Mendoza, Argentina, in 1971 into a family of Lebanese immigrants. In 1998 he graduated as a lawyer from the Law School of the National University of Cuyo. Since then, he has worked as an adviser to various associations, factories, workshops, companies and aeronautical organisations. In parallel, Gustavo is a professor of Aeronautical Law at four Argentine universities. He has published more than 200 investigations and has given more than 100 conferences on different topics related mainly to the Argentine Civil Aviation. He actively collaborates with the Argentine Association of Space Technology and the Mars Society Argentina. He is founder and partner of the aerospace consultancy MACK Aerospace Consulting SRL.

The author reviewing the secret telegrams sent to and from the Foreign Ministry of Argentina, after the downing of the Canadair CL-44 over Armenia, in the Archive of the Ministry of Foreign Affairs and Worship, in Puerto Nuevo de Buenos Aires, Terminal 5, Dock F, in 2015. (Guido Chiretti)

The Condor Building, headquarters of the General Staff of the Argentine Air Force, photographed from the intersection of Pedro Zanni and Avenida de los Immigrantes, in the Autonomous City of Buenos Aires. In its basement, in 2013, thousands of secret documents related to the performance of the institution during the National Reorganisation Process, would be found. (Alejandro Goldenberg)

After the discovery of secret documents in the basement of the Condor Building, the Ministry of Defence of Argentina started the Open Archives programme, by virtue of which their organisation, declassification, organisation and availability took place. Thanks to this material, it became possible to reconstruct the last years of Transporte Aéreo Rioplatense and the role that the Argentine Air Force played. (Author's collection)